The Nipper

CHARLIE MITCHELL

The Nipper

The heartbreaking true story of a little boy and his
violent childhood in working-class Dundee

HarperElement
An Imprint of HarperCollins*Publishers*
77–85 Fulham Palace Road,
Hammersmith, London W6 8JB

The website address is: www.harpercollins.co.uk

and *HarperElement* are trademarks
of HarperCollins*Publishers* Ltd

First published by HarperElement 2008

1

© Charlie Mitchell 2008

Charlie Mitchell asserts the moral right to
be identified as the author of this work

A catalogue record of this book is
available from the British Library

ISBN 978-0-00-729259-2

Printed and bound in Great Britain by
Clays Ltd, St Ives plc

Mixed Sources
Product group from well-managed
forests and other controlled sources
www.fsc.org Cert no. SW-COC-1806
© 1996 Forest Stewardship Council

FSC is a non-profit international organisation established to promote the
responsible management of the world's forests. Products carrying the FSC
label are independently certified to assure consumers that they come
from forests that are managed to meet the social, economic and
ecological needs of present and future generations.

Find out more about HarperCollins and the environment at
www.harpercollins.co.uk/green

In loving memory of Shane,
the nicest and funniest person
I have ever had the pleasure to meet.
I'll see you again one day.
Your big cuz, Milky Mitchell

Foreword

I am an optimist and believe that everyone deserves a second chance in life. But I also believe that some people, such as my father, are evil to the point of insanity and beyond help. I am sure when you read what happened to me as a child you will understand what I mean.

For years I have tried to work out the reason for his behaviour towards me and have never come up with an answer. I've put it down to a chemical imbalance in his brain. Like being born without that cut-off switch that tells you right from wrong. These kinds of people know what they are doing is wrong but don't care. And they use alcohol or drugs as an excuse to hide the fact that they actually enjoy it.

If you drink or take drugs, you do turn into a different person. But it's not an excuse. You make your own life choices. And if you turn into a monster when you fill your body with these things, then it's your responsibility to stop taking them. Life is really hard sometimes and every choice you make determines your future, and everyone is capable of making the wrong choices at some point in their life. The main thing is that you learn from your mistakes. Because one day your freedom may be taken away, or even worse, your life.

This book will show you the devastating effects child torture can have on a kid. It will make you sad and make you laugh and sometimes will make you dislike me. I'm in no way proud of any of the stories in this book, and I just hope that people can understand why I was like the way I was. My main aim is to show young people who are thinking of choosing the life I did what the consequences are. And to show people that no matter how close you are to death and giving up, there is always a chance that you can turn your life around.

In life, every decision you make has an outcome, some good and some bad, and there are always two roads you can take. I always chose the wrong road, as my anger or need for attention would make the choice easy. But over the years I have realised that I was using my childhood as an excuse for everything I did. A large part was my father's fault, but a lot of it was down to the roads I chose.

Drugs and drink were my choice, and the violence that followed was caused by my decision to take them, as they would trigger memories of my childhood. I just pray that after you read this book, you will forget about being a victim, and start thinking about what is good in your life – what you can achieve and how you are going to make the most of what you have.

My advice to people who read this book is to think seriously before you live the life that I did. Who cares if all your friends are on drugs, or fighting every night? They can't help you when you stand in front of a judge, or are struggling to pay the bills when you're older.

And no matter what you go through in life, don't use it as an excuse to self-destruct. Ask someone for help. Because the longer you let things happen, the more you'll accept it as normal life.

Life is never over till the fat lady sings. Unless, she falls out of a window and lands on you.

Life is never easy, but if you think about famine, war and all the other terrible things that are happening in the world, it puts it into perspective. Having to pay bills, or arguing over *EastEnders* or your team losing a football match is not the end of the world.

Treat people the way you want them to treat you. The better the person you become, the easier your life becomes. Well, that's all I have to say at the moment, except … welcome to Dundee.

Prologue

Through a small gap in the curtains I can see the snow floating gently past the street lamp. Trying to focus my eyes, I yawn. It's the middle of the night and I've been woken up by the sound of shouting and swearing from the living room. A few moments later the bedroom door opens.

'Come on you – get up.' He's dragging me out of the bed by my arm and yanking me down the corridor and into the kitchen as he sways from side to side. The smell of cigarette smoke and beer and vodka turns my stomach, as I'm now in his arms, and only inches from his scarred face.

'What is it, Dad? Is something wrong?'

'Wrong? No nothing's wrong. I've made yi a cup o' tea. Yi like tea, don't yi?'

He pushes me down on the chair and starts to boil the kettle. Why has he woken me up like this and why do I have to drink tea?

I don't even like tea. But I don't dare say anything. Besides I'm shivering as it feels like it's minus ten degrees. It's one of the coldest nights on record in Dundee and I'm dressed only in my old paisley pyjamas that are already two sizes too small for me.

'What's the matter, son? Are yi cald?'

'Yeah, it's freezing,' I reply as my teeth rattle together.

'This'll warm yi up then.'

He turns back to the stove, pours the boiling water from the kettle into a cup.

The next few seconds seem to happen in slow motion.

As he turns round again I think he's going to hand me the cup but instead he reaches across to me and there's something in his hand but it's not a cup and a second later I feel an agonising, scalding sensation that starts in the middle of my cheek, spreads across my whole body and then seems to shoot into my heart.

Dad has pressed a burning teaspoon on my face and he's holding it there long enough to get a result – he's scored a goal and he grins because he can see that I'm in agony as I've started screaming out in pain.

'Oh, is it too hot for yi, pal? Sorry, son, this'll cool it doon.'

He looks straight into my eyes and then spits right into my face, his saliva mixing with the tears running down my cheeks.

Dad grins again and takes a swig of his vodka.

I'm just a nipper, and I'm frightened and I don't understand. But I am still too young to realise what the effect of living with Dad is going to have on my life; too young to know that I will live the majority of my childhood as a virtual prisoner, and that my home in the Dundee tenements will be my torture den.

And it has only just begun . . .

The Nipper

Chapter One

First Day, No Way

It's 1980 and a freezing September morning in a run-down tenement block in St Fillans Road in St Mary's, Dundee. The winner takes it all, the loser has to fall … Snow is driving horizontally against the misty bedroom window and the Abba record has been repeating all night in the living room.

The time on my Mickey Mouse clock says 7.30 and it's my first day at school – I'm nearly five years old and I can't wait to meet new friends and play snowball fights with the kids I'll meet. I'm a cheerful kid by nature, and as soon as I get out of my prison I always feel happy and excited and free.

I'm trying not to make too much noise getting up, as I don't want to wake Dad. He's probably not long fallen asleep. My head is pounding and my eyes have not yet fully opened as the swelling from last night's head blows is dropping down my face and into my eyes.

I've opened my creaky bedroom door to go to the toilet, trying not to step on any loose floorboards in case Dad wakes up. The house is freezing and I'm shivering in my brown and yellow Y-fronts, the wind blowing through every nook and cranny in the door and windows.

I close the door and to my relief make it to the toilet, passing a broken mirror on the left-hand wall; I can only see the top of my head, so I stand on the side of the bath and stretch over with one hand on the sink, and peer in. I have never seen before what I see this morning – the shape and colour of what used to be my face is like a Freddy Krueger Halloween mask.

There is dried blood in the corner of both my eyes, and my neck has three long gashes down the back of my ear to my shoulder. My temples are swollen so badly that I can hardly see my ears. Then that creepy deep voice comes from the other side of the door.

'*Charlie! What are you doing in there?*'

'Nothing, Dad! I'm coming now! I'm brushing my teeth!'

'Good lad, hurry up – I'm bursting for a piss.'

'OK, Dad!' I can hear him coughing his lungs up as he walks back up the hall towards the kitchen to release last night's cigarettes into the sink.

Now I'm thinking, *Why is he being nice?* I thought he was annoyed with me after last night! … Maybe he didn't mean to hit me. I open the door and he's standing with his back to

2

me in the hall, scratching his head with one hand and his arse with the other. He's still a bit pissed from last night, I think.

'First day of school today, son.' He turns around slowly. 'Get your clothes – oh, what the fuck has happened to you? *Jesus Christ*, your face, who the fuck did that?'

He looks angry, as if about to pop.

'You, Dad! You told me to go to bed last night, and when I woke up you were punching me in the face for shouting and making a noise.'

I had obviously had a nightmare and must have been shouting in my sleep.

There's a silence for about two minutes as he walks into the bathroom with his head in his hands. He sits on the edge of the bath and mutters something along the lines of, *Please no again! Fuck no! Fucking hell!* He turns to me with a confused look on his face.

'Go back to bed, son, you don't have to go to school, I'll ring them and tell them you're ill. Go on! Everything's a'right, Charlie, close the door, son.'

I close the door and go back into my bedroom, totally confused at what has just happened. Did he batter me last night, or was it a dream? It's absolutely freezing, so I'm just glad to get back into the warmth of my bed, avoiding the damp patch where I pissed it with fear the night before.

I lie down, pull the cover over myself and rest my head on the pillow, trying to work out what's going on.

'Ouch!' I have to sit back up, as my head feels as if it's in a vice when my temples hit the pillow.

I will never forget this pounding in my skull. It's like having a heartbeat in my head, or in a cartoon when you watch someone hit their thumb with a hammer and it starts throbbing. I can't sleep even though I am tired, so I climb back out of bed and walk over to the bedroom window to see if the snow is deep enough to build a snowman if I manage to get out later. It has gone off a bit and isn't beating against the window any more, but it's really deep, as it has been falling all night. I can see my downstairs neighbour with his mum and dad sliding him down the road with one hand each – on his way to school, I bet.

I really want to be out there and on my way with him, but no such luck. The state my face is in, I'm definitely not going out, as I look like I've just gone ten rounds with Mike Tyson.

I hear Dad on the phone to school, telling them I have sickness and diarrhoea and that I'll be in as soon as I'm better, then I hear the floorboards creak as he walks back towards my bedroom door. I quickly lie back on the bed and wait for him to come in, praying that he's actually sorry and not coming back to finish me off.

You see, you never know with Dad. He can change in seconds. But although I've always known that he can be really scary after what he did to Mum and Mandy, this is the first time he's done it to me, the first time he's battered me. Even though I want to think I dreamt it, I know it really happened. I'm terrified that it will happen again and I'm now seeing Dad with new eyes. There's always been something about him when he's drunk that has frightened me, but he's never taken it out on me like this before. Overnight my dad has become a scary monster and it's something I'll never forget for the rest of my life.

The door opens, then he comes and sits next to me on the bed.

'I'm really sorry, son, I can't remember what happened.' Then he puts his fingers on the side of my head and strokes it softly. 'That will never happen again, son, I promise.'

'It's OK, Dad, I know you didn't mean it.'

That isn't what I'm thinking but he doesn't have to know that.

'Come on, son. I'll make your breakfast – come through.' He stands up and walks out of the bedroom.

I go through into the living room and sit on the couch next to the window, looking around the room. When I think back to it, I can't imagine how he coped with a hangover looking at that crazy interior car crash of the early Eighties. That's probably why he ended up as an alcoholic: he couldn't handle walking into the front room sober, as the décor would have made him vomit.

We live on the middle floor of a grey, unloved three-storey tenement, up pee-stained steps to the front door. There's a mouldy, dingy smell from the rotten carpet in the bathroom, the cluttered kitchen is further up, then three bedrooms and the living room at the end of a long corridor which I call the 'Hall of Imminent Death'. It has cold, creaky floorboards and feels like a dungeon, very dark and grey. The dirty carpet and peeling wallpaper in the living room are flower-patterned but, bizarrely, totally different in colour: the wallpaper's green and orange while the carpet is yellow and brown.

The living room has a two-bar electric fire with the grid broken off the front and the atmosphere's always smoky from Dad's cigarettes and butt-filled ashtrays. He makes new fags out of the butts with Red Rizla cigarette papers when he runs out of his ciggies. The TV in the corner is always on – if the money in the meter on the back of it hasn't run out.

The L-shaped couch I'm sitting on takes up a fair share of the room. We got it from MFI. It has great big chunky square arms and is covered in some kind of potato sack material with a diagonal plum-coloured stripe, though it's mainly faded to grey. This couch is where I spend most of my childhood getting battered.

The windows are black inside and out from never being cleaned, but it doesn't really matter as there's not much to see out of them – just the main road and a couple of semi-detached houses opposite.

Dad hoovers now and again but it's rarely clean or tidy and there are always rings on the table from coffee cups. Even when Mandy stays, he does most of the cooking. We mainly eat chips, fish fingers and beans on toast, which is my favourite. ('We had toast *and* beans, how posh are we?')

I don't have a bedtime. He doesn't care what time I get to bed. Most nights when he's drunk I want to go to bed but daren't ask.

He'll be sitting there dozing off with the telly on and then it will turn into that high-pitched whistle, or sometimes I'll sit with him not daring to move, watching the Test Card with the girl holding the stuffed clown for hour after hour. We stick a quid in the meter and when that runs out he'll just sit there swearing like a trooper for hours, but as always I don't dare move.

However drunk he is, he never spills his drink. His head may be touching the floor but the hooligan soup – his vodka – will be intact.

Even if he's hammered he'll be on his best behaviour if I have friends over, but if they go to the toilet he'll give me that snide look once they're out of the room and will start swearing nastily. He's able to control it though, and that's why I know it isn't just the drink that makes him do all the things he does to me.

Dad comes through from the kitchen with my toast and beans and a glass of water. There's a fuzzy half-screen cartoon on the telly.

'Here you are, son. I'll be back shortly, I'm just nipping to the shops for milk.'

That means vodka – I'm not that daft.

'See yi in a minute, Dad.'

The door closes and I start the difficult task of eating toast with lips like Mick Jagger's. My jaw's aching as well but nothing is going to stop me wolfing it down, as you can be sure that food is never spilling out of the cupboards in our house. You have to eat while you can, as you never know when it will be there again. It takes a few days for the swelling to go down and bruising to turn yellow and descend towards my cheeks, but I don't care as I just want it to go, so I can get out into the snow and start school. Anything to get me out of this hellhole. I'm sure it's colder in here than outside. The joys of living in a council flat.

My dad Jock is a big stout bloke in his early thirties, with dark curly hair and a squashed nose from getting it broken seven times. He's always had a beard and moustache; sometimes it's just stubble, but he's never clean-shaven. His front teeth are like fangs, as he has broken his jaw three or four times and had it wired up with these strange-looking disc things that look like shirt buttons. He has a scar on his left cheek where one of his mates smashed a pint glass in it during a punch-up in the local pub (the Pheasant, I think it was called). He has big hands with great thick fingernails and massive footballer's legs, and there's a huge scar on his thigh where he had to have pins put in because someone ran him over after he had tried to run Mum over when she was seven months pregnant.

He's a Jekyll and Hyde character, my dad. One minute he's happy, asking me if I want to go camping, then in a flash

8

he's snapping about dishes not being done, or my bed not being made. Literally before he has taken a breath. It's very confusing for me as a kid, as I have to adjust my thinking to cope with two different people, even though I only live with one. I don't understand why he changes so quickly and there's no one to help me deal with it. I'm on my own with him and I'm always scared of him.

Everyone who knows him says he's one of the funniest blokes they've ever met, but a lot of them don't know how mean and scary he really is behind closed doors. I, on the other hand, am a little short arse with fair mousy brown hair, and freckles on my cheeks and nose. Three foot nothing, built like the gable end of a pound note, with a home-made hair-cut that Worzel Gummidge's idiot child would complain about and dressed in naff clothes that Dad buys me in jumble sales and bargain stores. Eighties tat.

Today I'm wearing a maroon jumper with patches on the elbows, Farah's Sta-Press trousers with itchy wool, shoes that are at least one size too big from British Home Stores. Most of the time I wear hand-me-downs from Dad's friends' kids or from my Aunt Molly's kids or from Barnardo's, the char-ity shop in Reform Street. He gets a grant from the social to buy clothes – he sells it on sometimes for drink but will always make sure I have clothes for the start of the year – like today was going to be. He never takes me out shopping – he just gets the clothes on his own, which is why they're always too big or too small. He mostly gets them bigger and says I'll grow into them. It doesn't matter to him that my shoes look like hand-me-downs from Coco the Clown.

I've also got some other footwear – some sand shoes like plimsoles and a pair of monkey boots, shaped like a meat pastie in front, with stitching like an Eskimo had got his hands on them.

People I know go snowdropping – that's nicking off other people's washing lines – but they leave clothes on our washing line. I remember one of Dad's mates saying, 'Jock, if your house was burgled they'd probably leave you a fiver and their shoes.'

It isn't just us that are skint though: everyone's in the same boat. They joke about it bitterly in the pub. Dad sometimes takes me in there with him.

'What will the nipper have?' one of his drinking pals will say.

'Charlie will have what I have,' he replies, but then gives a broad wink.

I sip a Coca Cola while he drinks his vodka and I listen to them all trading hard luck stories and generally having a moan. One of Dad's friends says that when he has a bath he's so poor he has to wash the dishes in there with him to save on water, with all the bacon and eggs floating around in his lukewarm bathwater.

The men in the pub drink their pints and moan and groan about the English and the state of the world. The English they call bloody animals, the police are bastards, the vatman's a pig, the taxman's a cunt – as if any of them have ever paid tax or VAT in their lives. All Dad's friends spend all day in the pub and most of that time is spent talking about the English, but I don't think they've ever even met an Englishman. They seem to have it in for the English, though, mainly because of a woman called Maggie Thatcher.

Dad blames everything on Maggie Thatcher. I used to think she was the old witch at number 47, the one with the moustache who stabs every ball that goes in her garden. But now I know who she really is. She's a burglar from another rough area, who comes out at night and steals everyone's worldly belongings.

Chapter Two

A Fairy Tale of Dundee

*B*efore I say what happens next, I need to tell you how all this began. I still don't understand most of what went on when I was two years old, but I've managed to piece together what happened from my mum and from other people who knew how it was.

The story began around 1972 in Dundee on the east coast of Scotland, when a sixteen-year-old girl called Sarah (my mum) – who had just left school – met a twenty-one-year-old lad called Jock (my dad) from St Mary's in Dundee. Mum was beautiful with blue eyes, a pale freckled face and long blonde hair which she wore in a fringe. She came from a decent family and was the middle of six children – with four brothers and one sister.

He was a strong, handsome lad, of average height and powerfully built. He also had blue eyes, dark curly hair and tanned skin from time spent outdoors. He was a promising footballer – his father had played for Dundee United – and he had three sisters and one brother.

They had been introduced to each other by mutual friends at a house party and hit it off straight away. He was a live wire, always cracking jokes, never serious for a minute. He was instantly drawn to her: she was very pretty, warm and bubbly – she loved to laugh and to make other people laugh. They were quite similar people back then, and at first they looked like a match made in heaven.

In the late Sixties, early Seventies, Dundee was a very poor city. Everyone seemed to be unemployed and there wasn't a lot of things to do. Money was scarce. But they never thought about problems like that as they had found true love. They dated for a couple of years and things were going fantastically. He was always the life and soul of the party, and she loved her life with him, as he always had her in fits of laughter with his childish antics.

They decided to move in together as they were both happy and life was a breeze. They got married quite quickly and moved to a derelict flat up a back alley off Hilltown, a big road that goes right through Dundee. The street – Arkly Street – was a row of terraced houses like Coronation Street, with a welder's yard and scrapyard at the end. The roofs were crooked and had sunk over the years.

They stayed there for twelve months. The odd argument occurred, but as my Uncle Danny used to say (that's my dad's younger brother), 'Show me a couple that doesn't argue and I'll buy you a pint – and that's a lot coming from a Scotsman.'

Then Mum fell pregnant in March 1973 with her first child, Tommy, born in December 1973, and again two years later in late January 1975 with her second, Charlie – that's me. I was born in November of that year.

In between those two years Mum started to notice a big change in Dad. He was getting more aggressive and argumentative towards her. He would get jealous for no reason at all, and had even taken to locking her in when he went out to the pub. She had seen him fighting with men in town some nights, but that was normal in Dundee at this time. Men sorted everything out with a punch-up at the end of the night if they had a grievance. That's just the way it was.

But Mum never thought that Dad would ever turn his anger on her, as they were meant to love each other. And people that are in love don't lift their hands to each other. Dad obviously had a different view of love, as he was now coming home drunk and beating her and accusing her of having an affair with anyone who looked at her. He was gradually turning into a possessive, aggressive control freak who needed professional help.

The level of the beatings and mental torture he was giving Mum was beyond belief. He would keep her up for hours, snapping questions at her like an interrogation agent, then kick and punch and sometimes bite her.

* * *

I have a recurring nightmare right through my early childhood. I'm hiding in the corner, crouched under a table, terrified. I see what he's doing to her and I can see clumps of her hair on the floor.

'Yi fuckin' bitch, yi think yi can pull the wool over my eyes?' He's dragging my mum across the room by her hair, kicking her in the ribs and stomach. He's pulling all her hair out and she's screaming and whimpering, bent over in agony, desperately trying to defend herself.

I want to look away but I can't and the scene is branded in my memory forever.

'Please stop it, Jock, let me go. I hav'na done anything.'

'I hav'na done anything. I hav'na done anything,' he mocks. 'Yir just the innocent victim, eh?'

'Yi ken I am, Jock.'

'Yir a fuckin' liar, that's what yi are.'

He punches her in the face and I can't bear to hear her screams.

'Now are yi gonna start tellin' me what's really going on, yi fuckin' slut!'

'Nothing, Jock, nothing's going on.'

'Nothing, eh? So who wiz that fella eyein' ye up yesterday – Mr Fuckin' Nobody I suppose, or scotch mist maybe?'

He's now in such a rage that I put my hands over my ears. I want it all to stop.

'It's all right, Charlie,' says Tommy, who's crouched next to me. 'It's all right,' he says comforting me. 'Go back to sleep.'

That's when I wake up …

* * *

As I've said, living in Dundee it was the norm for men to be fighting every night. Women were used to seeing men beating each other up. But Dad had never given Mum the impression that he'd do that to her from the bond they'd had with each other. So when he started viciously beating her up and trying to take control of every part of her life, it took her completely by surprise. What's more, she never knew how and when nasty Jock would appear, as there were never any warning signs. He would suddenly just switch.

It was really hard for women back in those days in Scotland: the men had control over them and everyone seemed to accept that if a man battered a woman, it was none of their business. It was a domestic and that made it acceptable. When I was a little older it turned my stomach to think of the many nights of torture Mum had gone through alone, and it infuriated me that no one ever helped her.

He'd go to the pub, she'd be in with the kids, he'd come home, beat her up and say she'd been trying to sleep with the neighbour, or the postman, or any man within a two-mile radius. At first it was more verbal bullying and mental torture, and then it got worse with beatings and thrashings. She couldn't even go to the shops for a pint of milk without being questioned for hours on her return – he battered her so badly that he broke her teeth and nose.

Over the next few months Mum started to become numb to the mental and physical torture she had to endure at the hands of Dad, but was becoming seriously worried about us kids, and the fact that one night he might throw one of us out of the window, as he threatened he would do on quite a few occasions if she left. That was another thing about Jock – he was a very clever man. He knew exactly what to say to get inside your head and make you so scared and confused that you couldn't think for yourself. Mum was now waiting for the chance to leave; she had been trying to hatch a plan for a while, but was too afraid of the consequences if he caught her sneaking out.

Finally Mum decided she'd had enough. Dad regularly went down to the benefits office to claim dole as he was officially unemployed, although everyone knew he worked as a roofer and chimney sweep. One night while he was at work, Mum seized her chance. A few nights previously he had broken her ribs and she had to go to hospital – and that was the last straw for her.

She grabbed a few nappies, and things that were close to hand, and managed to sneak out. Standing in a bus shelter on Hilltown that night, cradling us from the pouring rain, with tears and mascara running down her face, she swore to herself she would never go back to him. But there was still the problem of us kids. Dad was never going to let her leave and take his kids as well – no chance!

Even though he didn't want us, he would still not let her have us. As it turned out, he was at least partly successful, as within a short while he managed to get me back.

And whatever inner turmoil, despair and anger he was going through, he would make me pay for it for many years to come.

Chapter Three

Tug of War

In 1976 after the breakup Mum and Dad started a three-year tug of war over us kids. There were doors kicked in, fights between uncles and aunts. One incident in particular stuck in my mind and later on in life made me realise that he never just flipped overnight but that he had always been an evil bastard.

I'm aged about three and Mum is at the social security sorting out her family allowance when out of the corner of her eye she spots Dad. Unfortunately they have both been booked for appointments in the same building at the same time. Mum's heart sinks at the sight of him but there's no place to run. Then Dad looks right at her and walks towards her with that evil smirk that she knows so well by now. As he approaches he doesn't do much at first, just asks how she is and how we are.

After a short conversation Dad asks if he can hold me, as Tommy's now hiding behind Mum's leg with a plastic gun pointed at Dad, saying. 'No Dad, go away.'

I can see in an instant the look of fear and hesitation in Mum's face and then she's handing me over to Dad and he's grabbing me like I'm a rag doll. I'm scared, but mainly because I can see that Mum's starting to cry and it's making me cry too and I try to reach out to Mum, but Dad's now holding me in a tight grip and won't let go, even though he has sworn on us boys' lives that he'll give me back to her. Then that look comes back on his face and the voice she's been so scared of reappears.

'Do yi really think yir getting the nipper back, you bitch?'

Mum now realises that he's again managed to twist her mind and sneak under her guard, this time bargaining with our lives.

He's far too strong for Mum as he's a big lump of a man and she is small and petite. Mum is now screaming at the top of her lungs, pleading and begging Dad to give me back to her, but Dad just stands there laughing at her, as he gets off on things like this – you know, watching people beg.

'Please, Jock, geeze um back.'

'If yi come back ti the hoose now, y'ill git yir bairn back.'

'Kin yi jist hand 'im back in case yi drap um.'

'*Fuck off yi cow!* If yi want um, come and git um.'

He pretends to drop me.

'Oh, do yi want yir bairn?'

By now he's taken me out of the social security office and we're on the street. He carries me into the middle of the road and then puts me down between the two lanes of traffic, as cars swerve to miss me. I'm lying there, petrified, listening to the screeching of brakes and car horns hooting at me but I'm unable to move, confused about what's happening.

'*Mum ... Dad!*' I start to wail and scream.

'*Help!*' Mum screams. '*Somebody please help!* Look what he's dain ti mi bairn!'

Everyone just walks past, not batting an eyelid. It's in the middle of town first thing in the morning and not one person even stops to ask her what is going on.

Dad picks me back up off the road and points at Tommy.

'I'll be back fir him the morin tae, yi fucking bint.'

He's holding me in one hand and has a cigarette in the other. Mum stands there screaming and begging passers-by to help, but her pleas fall on deaf ears.

Dad is now turning to walk away, throwing his Regal King Size towards her. Mum has no choice but to go back with him. Even though she knows he might kill her this time, the thought of leaving me with him is too much to take.

'Jock, wait, I'm coming!'

He turns around with that evil smirk on his face. 'I thought yi might.'

She walks up towards the house behind him, and is now trying to devise a plan. She will go back, take a beating, then earn his trust. That way she can wait until he's at the pub and move us somewhere far away from there before he gets home.

As for me, I'm getting used to this constant snatching of me by one or other of my parents. It's like they're using me as a toy, a possession that both of them want. When you're growing up, you're learning to talk, learning to walk. I'm not – I'm just getting dragged around all over the place, listening to women getting beaten up.

I'm almost expecting Dad to snatch me away from Mum or Mum to grab me again. There is no such thing as routine in my life, as I never know whose house I might wake up in, who will be feeding me or putting me to bed, or whether I'll get a bedtime story, although on the whole I'm spending more time with Dad than Mum so bedtime stories are definitely out of the question, apart from stories that begin with a clip round the head and end in being kicked around the house.

Apparently at one point when I'm just one year old my dad even holds me out of a window in an apartment seventeen storeys up – it's my Michael Jackson moment – and says:

'Do yi want me to let your fuckin' son go?'

I later find out that from the age of six or seven months if Mum left the room, I'd start to cry. She'd come back in and say to Dad, 'What are yi doing to him?'

So at that early age I must have been very attached to Mum – and also aware of what Dad was capable of doing to me.

* * *

About a week after Dad snatched me from Mum in the social security office, he decided to go out with one of his mates, as Mum had lured him into a false sense of security – a trick that she'd picked up from years of living with him.

I was in bed, but not asleep, listening to the sound of the evening traffic, when I heard her jewellery clanging and footsteps approaching the bedroom door. I knew it was her, I knew the sound of her heels on the creaky floorboards.

'Wake up, Charlie,' she whispered. 'We'll be goin' to meh hoose. Wir goin' on an adventure. But we'll have to hurry up so come on – get your coat on, pal.'

She helped me dress and then packed a few clothes and I picked up Boris, my old one-eyed bear, and we walked out of Arkly Street, ready for a new life, a fresh start. Anywhere would do, as long as she never had to see his evil, scarred face again.

What Mum hadn't counted on, though, was just how selfish and unsupportive the people around her could be: nobody wanted to get involved in this nightmare in which she was now living. There she was – two kids, no house, and no money for food in the freezing cold winter with a paranoid schizo wanting her dead.

My Aunty Molly (Dad's sister) took Mum in for a while and a little later she met a man called Blake. He was a quiet, introverted man with a moustache and glasses, but he was actually very tough, an ex-soldier. You wouldn't want to meet him up a dark alley. But at the same time he was very gentle and protective towards women.

Mum stayed at Blake's mum's house for two weeks while waiting on the council to give her a flat. But three weeks after Mum had escaped from Arkly Street Dad snatched us back. Blake was out in town somewhere with his mates and Mum was working that night, waitressing at a café up the road. Dad simply walked through the back door of Blake's mum's house and crept upstairs to the bedroom where we were asleep.

We woke up, dazed and confused about what was happening, until we felt Dad's clawlike nails digging into our arms as he dragged us out of bed. We both of us cried and whimpered as we realised who it was, but he ignored us and hurried down the stairs past Blake's mum who tried to stop him in the hall, but he grabbed her hair and shoved her out of the way and walked off with us into the dark, cold night.

Over the next two years Tommy and I were stolen back and forward at least five times. Every time Dad or Mum spotted the other one out in town, they tried to steal us back. Sometimes it was when Dad was working, or when we had babysitters looking after us.

On one occasion in town Dad saw Mum with us, pushing the buggy, and grabbed both of us but Tommy managed to wriggle free and ran through town, finding his way back to Mum.

Most of Mum's time was spent trying to think of ways to get us back without getting her face smashed in by Dad. She had been trying to get her life back on track and now had a flat of her own. She lived with Blake in a council flat in Princess Street on Hilltown. In 1979 she married Blake and had his baby, my half brother Bobby. Years later I discovered that Dad had tried to run Mum over when she was seven months pregnant with Bobby.

At that stage Mum hadn't been seeing Blake that long and didn't really know that much about him – only that he was a nice, well-spoken man, really easy-going, totally the opposite of Dad.

Mum never mentioned her troubles to Blake, as she was scared what Dad might do to him if he got involved. What none of us – Mum, Tommy and me – knew until later was that Blake might be nice and polite to women and kids, but with fully grown men it was a different story. He could handle himself.

Blake walks into the bathroom one night, as he can hear Mum crying.

'What's up love?'

'I'm worried aboot mi bairns, that bastard is probably hittin thum.'

'Wha's hittin yir bairns?'

'My ex-husband, Jock.'

'Put yir coat on and wi'll go an git thum.'

'Are you aff yir hade?'

'What are yi on aboot, if yi want them back, lets git thum.'

'It's Jock Mitchell, yi maniac, ir you mad?'

'Jock Shmock – come on, git yir coat on.'

Mum is now petrified. Even saying his name sends shivers down her spine. Blake walks back in with her coat as Mum looks at him in amazement.

'If we go up there, promise me you winna let him hit me.'

'He winna go near yi, come on.'

All Mum can think is that Dad will batter Blake, just like he's battered her. And as no one has ever helped her before, she is now brainwashed into thinking he is more powerful than the devil. Even so, this is too good an opportunity to let pass, so she jumps in the car and heads off on her latest mission to get Tommy and me back. All the way up there in the car she keeps asking Blake, 'Are yi sure yi kin fight now? What if he hits me? What if he's got a gun?'

Blake just turns and smiles. 'He winna lay a finger on yi, trust me.'

They stop outside the house, get out of the car, then open the front door and walk in. Mum is now digging her nails into Blake's arm and shaking uncontrollably with fear, as Dad walks out of the kitchen and sees them standing there.

'What the fuck ir you dain' in meh hoose, and wah the fuck is he?'

'Never mind wah eh am,' says Blake. 'Get yir bairns, Sarah.'

Mum is now trembling with fear at the sight of Dad. 'I canna, he's gonna hit me.'

'You go near they bairns and I will hit yi,' Dad snaps.

'Do ya think so?' Blake snaps back.

Dad has walked back into the kitchen and comes out again holding a knife.

'What di yi think yir awa ti dae we that?'

'Fuck all, I'm fixin' a plug.'

The next minute Dad is sat back in the armchair with a broken jaw; Blake never gives him the chance to use the knife. As Dad has looked down, probably preparing one of his fly moves, Blake has booted him in the chin.

'If you ever pull a knife on me again, ya prick, I'll kill ya,' says Blake.

'The bairns are in the room. Eh dinna want this gittin' oot o' hand,' says Mum, who's starting to panic.

Tommy and I are upstairs asleep but the commotion wakes us up and we hear everything that's going on.

Mum is now confused at the situation, as she has never seen this side of Dad. He is now on the receiving end for a change. But she's still watching him like a hawk as this could be one of his tricks. And he still has the knife in his hand.

'Come back the mornin' and yi'll git thum back. Dinna wake thum up now.'

'Smack his puss, Sarah, fir a' the hidings he gave you. It's aright, he winna touch yi.'

'No let's get oot o' here in case the police 'ave been phoned.' She just wants out of there now, as she still doesn't think Dad's going to take what has just happened quietly.

They head off in the car and wait till the next morning to go back, but by that time Dad's long gone. He has taken us to Aunt Helen's house at the bottom of Lawhill (I play there with her kids, my cousins) and has then driven to hospital to get his jaw wired up. Mum only finds this out when she goes to my Nan's house looking for us, as she's greeted with a mouthful for what Blake did to Dad. I find that a bit weird as Nan knows what Dad's like from past experience. I suppose blood is thicker than water.

Mum split up with Blake a couple of years later but as the tug of war between her and Dad continued, with Tommy and me being the rope they were pulling on, I never really got to know him.

In retaliation for Dad's attempt on Mum's life when she was pregnant with Bobby, there was an attempt on Dad's life, when he was run over by a car as he walked out of a local pub. Dad got off lightly – just a few bruised ribs and minor injuries to the hip and shoulder which soon healed. He also had a twelve-inch gash to his leg which scarred it for life. He always claimed that Blake had something to do with this, but I think he just wanted to have another excuse to bully Mum.

He managed to snatch me again when I was approaching my third birthday and this time he headed over to the Isle of Man on the ferry, with me in tow …

I'm standing on the boat with him and it's cold and windy and I don't know whether I'll see Mum or Tommy again. I'm fishing off the side of the boat and catch a conger eel with this orange rope handline, given to me by Dad to keep me amused. It nearly pulls me into the water and the rope cuts through my hand … It's amazing that all of these fishermen have the best rods, reels and bait but catch nothing, and I have this silly little handline and I hook a thirty-pound conger.

But maybe it would have been better if the captain had never saved me from being dragged overboard – or maybe drowning me is Dad's plan …

His new life in the Isle of Man was cut short and he had to come back. I don't know why we only spent a few months there. I think he got kicked off the island for some reason, but he never told me why we came back.

Finally, when I was around three and a half years old and my big brother Tommy was five, they settled the custody battle in court.

Tommy and I are sitting there between Mum and Dad in a big, gloomy wood-panelled courtroom in Dundee. There's this musty smell of ancient wax polish, disinfectant and broken lives. I don't really know what's going on but a man in a wig who I learn later is the judge seems to be in a hurry for us to leave, as he keeps snapping questions at Mum and Dad. Maybe he wants his lunch. Then suddenly he's asking me who I want to live with, Mum or Dad.

By this time I've spent more of my life with Dad than I have with my mum and there doesn't seem to be any choice. Besides I'm too frightened to say anything else.

'Dad,' I mumble nervously.

'What's he saying?' says the judge.

'He wants to be with me, Yi Honour,' replies Dad, quickly and smartly.

Tommy has chosen Mum and in the next few minutes my childhood fate is sealed. The judge rules that I should live with Dad and Tommy should live with Mum. After all, it seems fair for both parents to have one kid each.

Mum's crying and calling Dad a bastard and shouting something about access but Dad just says, 'Yi can fuck off!' and walks out of the courtroom, taking me with him.

'Come with me, son. Come with me, son,' Mum's begging me as I follow my dad out. I feel stunned and miserable, and I'm trying not to listen too closely to her begging as it hurts too much. And even though I haven't spent much time with my mum over the last few years and I don't even feel I know her that well – she has already become a shadowy, distant figure in my life – I know I'm feeling that stab of pain in the pit of my tummy, a sense of isolation and terror, the same feeling

I had when Dad snatched me from the social security office and lay me in the middle of the traffic.

Only this time, I'm the one who's chosen not to be with my mum and I don't even know why, except that I'm too frightened of my monster-like dad to do anything else. And I'm worried that by choosing Dad over Mum, I've let her down. I'm thinking that the breakup of my parents' marriage must be my fault. I was the one who told the judge that I didn't want to go with my mum and so I must be the one who's to blame for her going out of my life.

I have been stolen back and forwards five times before by Dad and Mum, but this time Dad's stolen me for good. And this time I've let him steal me. I've chosen to live with him so I'm also to blame. But it's Dad who's won the tug of war – not me or Mum. Dad is an animal that Mum just can't handle. With him, it's like banging your head against a brick wall. No matter how hard you try, you can never win, and Mum has had the last bit of fight knocked out of her. She has her consolation prize: at least she's got Tommy, her first born.

As for me, now that I'm with Dad full-time I keep trying to imagine what it would have been like if I had replied 'Mum' to the judge not 'Dad', and if I had managed to escape along with Tommy that time he wriggled free of Dad in town. It's a hard thing to say but I've wished so many times that I had been the one to go with Mum, not Tommy.

I'm not yet four years old and I won't see my mother and brother again for most of my childhood. Instead my consolation prize is to look forward to years and years of physical and mental torture from my dad.

And my prison sentence has only just begun. The minimum term of my sentence is the whole of my childhood – though it may last much longer and could even be for life.

Chapter Four

The Woman in the Bath

After Dad takes me away from that horrible courtroom and now that he has complete custody over me, I know that I won't see my mum again. I know this because Dad keeps telling me.

'She's washed her hands of yir for good this time, the fuckin' bitch,' he smirks and of course I believe him. How can I not believe him? How can I know that she's crying for me every day? How am I to know that losing me is the worst thing that has ever happened to her and that she will spend the rest of my childhood years trying to get me back? I only find this out years later and by then the damage of our being torn apart has well and truly been done.

But for me, as a boy of less than four years old, out of sight means out of mind. Besides, Dad has told me that if Mum gets her hands on me again she'll try to kill me. She must be worse than Dad, I tell myself. After all, how can I know otherwise? And very soon I simply stop thinking about her.

After Dad and Mum broke up when I was ten months old, Dad had a short stint at the single life before he met a woman named Mandy. She's a really pretty woman from a big, well-known family in Dundee. By well known I mean that where we live in St Mary's, Dundee, everyone seems to know everyone else, especially when people come from big families. Mandy has three kids from her previous unhappy marriage, one girl and two boys, Julie, Paul and Peter. We all live together when I'm young.

Paul, who's the middle child and a year older than me, soon becomes my best friend, and our friendship continues for many years into adult life. And Julie and Peter will always be like a brother and sister to me.

By the time I'm five I'm already living in fear of what my dad will do to me. The first time he battered me was the night before what should have been my first day at school. I now look forward to the rare occasions when he leaves me with someone else when he goes off somewhere, and for a brief time I'm free from him, off the hook. Like the time he takes Mandy and her three kids to Blackpool and leaves me behind with one of the neighbours, so I can go and pick berries to make money over the holidays.

Although my memories of my mother are already growing hazy I remember how Dad used to beat her up and mentally torture her, so in a way I'm not surprised when he carries on doing this in his relationship with Mandy.

Night after night I'm forced to listen to the thuds and moans coming through the wall, until I fall asleep. I have a good idea what's going on, but I put the pillow over my head and cover my ears with my hands to block the noise out. I realise when I'm older that Mandy could have had anyone back then, as she was really good looking, but she ended up choosing a crazy aggressive thug with no morals or remorse for anything he did.

It's hard to explain how this could come about but I know people think that Dad has a really funny personality when they first meet him – and when he's sober. And the women he dates are led into a false sense of security by his happy-go-lucky attitude. But when he manages to get his feet under the table – once these women have let him into their lives and he's installed in their houses – he'll take to drinking and turn into an animal.

Even when I'm very young I know that he's using drink as an excuse to unleash the sadistic side of his nature that he can hide very well if it suits him, and that he enjoys inflicting pain – physical and mental, on people who are weaker than him.

There are many, many nights when I get dragged out of bed at three or four in the morning because Dad has beaten Mandy, and if he leaves, I have to leave as well.

Dad is a very sneaky man where women are involved. It's like he plans the beatings at certain times of the night, when the world has gone to sleep. And he will mostly aim for areas that can be covered up with clothes the next day. You'd know when he's really been pissed the night before because Mandy's face will be in a hell of a mess. I look at her sometimes, sitting on the couch with black eyes or burst lips, while he's whistling in the kitchen as if nothing has happened.

The bond that I have with Peter and Paul will never be broken. I may not see Paul for many years but I know he's always there for me and we're still like brothers when we meet up again. Mandy has always been there for me to talk to – but after she finally manages to get away from Dad I don't really see her that much, as my face is probably a constant reminder of what she went through at his hands.

Dad did a lot of bad things to Mandy in her life, but there is one particular night that scares the life out of me, a memory that I'll take to the grave. I'm staying in Mandy's house, and Dad wakes all the kids up including me, and tells us to come downstairs and watch.

'Everybody up, git up yi fuckers.' He's staggering around, pulling the bed covers off the beds. 'GET UP!'

He turns and walks back out of the room, while the four of us jump out of bed and run downstairs, where I can hear Mandy crying and pleading.

'No in front o' the bairns, please.'

We find them in the bathroom, where he has filled the bath to the top, and has Mandy by the hair, pushing her head under the water. We all realise at once that he's trying to drown her and he makes no secret of it either.

'Look at yir mum drooned.'

We all jump on his back and try to get him off. He pushes us away, but his rage seems to have subsided, as if he's achieved what he wanted – to scare the daylights out of Mandy, and us children too.

He leaves Mandy in the water, blue faced and bruised, and wanders off to the kitchen. I stand there in shock as I think she's about to die right in front of me. She eventually climbs out of the bath, shaken and shivering and hugging herself, grabbing a damp towel and retreating to her bedroom, as far away from him as possible.

I feel dreadful and guilty and ashamed, as if I've somehow colluded in what my dad has done to Mandy – after all, I am the spawn of this devil. I can never understand why nobody comes to help her but maybe he's got a spell over them like he has over me. He's so clever at concealing the truth. Maybe Mandy loves Dad that much that she never tells anyone – or maybe she's just like most women in Dundee and is used to being treated like a punch bag.

All in all Dad's with Mandy for five years – between when I'm two and seven. He finally beats her up once too often and she never comes back.

I miss her, as she's been like a mother to me. But I can't imagine how her children must be feeling, and even years afterwards I feel embarrassed even saying hello to her daughter in the street. I do stay in touch with Paul, though. We'll always be like brothers – and I still see him at school, as he's in the year above me.

Dad's beaten me many times between the ages of four and seven, but then Mandy's always been around to absorb some of the worst of his punches while I've been on what you might call the reserve bench.

Dad thought he had got Mandy where he wanted her. That's the kind of man he is: power mad, always wanting to be in control, and bullying people weaker than him. He's a hard man who will take on anyone, but as he gets older he seems to direct his obvious hate and anger at people who can't hit back.

And now that Mandy's gone, that can only mean me.

Chapter Five

The Monday Book

*I*n the tenement block I live in with Dad in St Fillans Road there are six flats in each block and three blocks joined onto each other. Everybody knows everybody; people will come to the door asking to borrow some sugar or you will be sent upstairs to borrow milk or a fag until Monday when the giro comes swooping through the letterbox.

Dad is on the dole but works as a roofer-come-chimney sweep – obviously illegally, but he never gets caught as the social never come into our area. I don't think they really give a monkey's about poor areas, as they have nothing to gain from them. The only people that knock on the door are debt collectors, people in suits looking for Dad. I'm turning into the best liar in Scotland, as Dad will send me to the door to tell them stories about him being at the hospital, or at the dentist. Then I'll come back into the living room, where Dad will be kneeling under the windowsill, looking out of a tiny gap in the curtains.

'They believed me, Dad.'

'Keep yir fucking voice doon, yi half-wit,' he'll whisper. Then he'll start the questioning, once they're out of sight.

'What did they want? What did you say? Then what did they say?'

I'm six years old by this time and I never really pay attention to what they're saying. I am more concerned about keeping them from pushing past me.

Between the age of five and seven, I learn how to keep on the good side of Dad. I will tell lies for him, keep lookout for men in suits when I'm out playing, and run to the shops for anything he needs. But I never know when he's going to give me a beating and they're getting worse. The first one he ever gave me – that meant I missed my first day at school – was just a taste of things to come. But today he takes it to a whole new level.

Dad has asked me to go and pick up his family allowance. He gives me the book for me to take to the post office and I then have to hand it over to the woman who'll tear a page out and give me his money. On this particular morning I am waiting in the queue among all the old biddies and single mums, right behind an old man in his sixties who has obviously lost control of his bowels, and must have eaten sprouts this morning. The air is toxic around me, and my height isn't helping at all. He smells like my neighbour's dog after it rains.

'Next please!'

Great, my turn. Thank God that windbag has gone – the air is so rife from his farts I can hardly see. I pull the book out of my pocket and hand it to the woman behind the counter.

'There yi go, misses.'

She is peering at me over her National Health glasses, with a plaster in the middle holding them together.

'Thank you son!'

She's now looking closely at the cover of the book.

'What's up with your dad's book? … All this black stuff on it, did he drop it?'

'No he left it in his pocket when he was sweeping chimneys.'

The place instantly goes silent. Well, how am I to know he isn't supposed to be working and claiming dole at the same time?

The woman behind the counter starts laughing. 'You're lucky I know your dad. You should be more careful who you say that to.'

Then all the people in the queue start laughing as I skip out of the door thinking I'm some kind of comedian. But I soon realise that Dad has a completely different sense of humour to me. I get back to the house white-knuckled from holding the money extra tight so I don't drop it, then go into the kitchen and hand it to Dad.

'There you go, Dad – sixty-nine pounds and thirty-eight pee.'

'What took yi so long? Yi've been fucking ages!'

41

'There was a massive queue, Dad, and some old woman was paying loads o' bills.'

'I'll go mi fucking self next time.'

Don't ask me to explain it, because I don't have a clue why my mouth opens and blurts out this next sentence. Maybe it's in case someone else tells him what went on, and then I wouldn't get a chance to explain myself.

'The woman asked in the post office why your book was black, and I told her it was soot from when you were sweeping chimneys, but she laughed!'

'Yi stupid little bastard!' I see his face change into a piercing, threatening stare as he puts his cup down on the kitchen worktop. I've never seen anyone's pupils go so big and black, I can see myself in them as he takes a step towards me, grinding his fanglike teeth.

'Come 'ere, yi little fucker.'

I walk backwards up the hall towards the living room with my hands up. 'Sorry Dad, sorry Dad, sorry Dad. Please I'm sorry.'

'Yi're sorry, are yi?' he says, walking towards me. Then *boot!* He kicks me right in the bollocks. I fall to the floor. Stamp! Stamp! Stamp! all over me, then he drags me up by the hair and throws me face-first into the wall. I fall onto the settee backwards screaming.

'Please stop, Dad, I'm sorry.' The egg on my forehead from the force of my face hitting the wall is now visible when I look up. 'Dad, I'll never do it again, I'm sorry, please, please, please – I'm sorry.'

I am now on my back with blood pouring down my face and into my eyes.

'If yi say I'm sorry once more I'll smother yi, yi little snivelling cunt. Shut it or I'll stop yi breathing.'

So I don't say another word. I just lie there like a dog on its back, with arms and legs in the air, sniffing and trying not to look at the massive egg-shaped bump on my forehead or say anything else that might start him off again.

'Get up, idiot. NOW! Get up!'

'Please Dad I'm sorry—'

'What did I tell you about saying yir sorry?' Smack! Smack! Bang! Bang! He just explodes again after pacing up and down the carpet, thinking about what it might mean for him to get caught by the social, I guess.

The beating goes on for around four hours. Dad covers my mouth to stop me screaming while smashing his head into my face and kneeing me in the groin. I can't even catch a breath as his hand is covering my mouth and nose. When I try to roll off the couch to get his hand away from my mouth, we both fall onto the floor, where he keeps smashing my head with a shoe, while clumps of my hair that he has been yanking out of my head are all over my face, and are now itching the hell out of my nose. My head feels like it's going to explode and my body is aching from the constant knee shots he is firing into it.

Suddenly he stops and gets up, walks out of the living room and into the kitchen, then comes back with a bottle of vodka and two litres of Coke. I feel like jumping through the window but we're three floors up and if it doesn't smash I know it will be ten times worse if I never get out.

'Get oot my fucking sight.'

I don't know whether I should move or if he is going to smash me on the way past so I just lie there, not moving from the position he left me, against the couch on the floor with my legs under the table.

'If I have to tell yi again, *fucking bed now.*'

So I jump up and chance it. He stands up as I try to run past and gives me one more boot in the back, sending me head first into the edge of the open door. That white flash I see when my skull smashes against the door will send a shiver down my spine for the rest of my life – and as an adult I still have the little indentation on my forehead from that cracked skull.

I drag myself off the floor, stagger into my room and close the door, just making it as I fall down face first onto the bed.

Blood is now pumping out of my head and covering the bed cover. It's about 9 p.m. and all I can hear is the lid from the vodka bottle being twisted back on, as I take the pillowcase off the pillow to press against my open wounds. I can hear the TV volume go down – he turned it up full blast earlier to drown out my screams. How nobody has come to the door this night I'll never know; I could have been murdered and people would have just sat at home with the telly turned up, so they didn't have to get involved. Bunch of cowards.

I stay up until about 5 a.m. waiting for round two, but it never comes. The pain is not the worst thing about tonight though; it's waiting for the bedroom door to open that really gets to me. My eyes will start to close, and then I hear movement, or he'll start singing along to music on the radio or one of his records at the top of his lungs.

Dad loves singing – especially if they're sentimental songs and he's drunk, and often when I hear them I'm crouched somewhere in the flat in pain and not daring to move. He's got old albums from the Sixties like the Kinks and the Rolling Stones, Tamla Motown, the Supremes and Stevie Wonder; and cassettes from the Seventies – he's always playing the Carpenters and Commodores and Abba; and then there's new, modern 1980s stuff like Alison Moyet and Lionel Richie. These records are the soundtrack of my childhood years of battering and abuse.

I'm completely exhausted but for eight hours that night I watch the door handle, listening to the odd can blowing down the street, cats fighting out the back green, police cars and ambulances going past but none stopping. I think that maybe someone may have called them to come and get him, but I am never that lucky.

The next day Dad says nothing to me in the morning. I am off school again but this time he's going to need a really good excuse as I'll be needing at least two weeks to recover because of the mess I'm in. But he's thought of something; I never find out what it is, but it works. He's a brilliant liar, you see, and has everyone under some kind of spell for years to come. As a six year old I'm desperate to tell someone, but I can't forget him telling me that if I ever tell anyone what's going on, he'll either kill me or my mum would get me – and she's fifty times worse, according to him.

Dad has told me that my mum tried to smother me just after I was born and that's why he had to keep stealing me off her. I'm finding it harder and harder to remember my mum so I'm starting to believe him – and I've had no contact with her or my brother Tommy since the day in the courtroom when I went off with Dad. He's also told me that she might kill me if she gets her hands on me again, and I sort of believe this too.

At least I think I do. He can make me think yes is no, up is down, black is white. I sometimes don't know what to believe. But I will end up believing what he wants me to believe just so that I can get some sleep.

Chapter Six

The Three Amigos

I go to school with my toes hanging out of the front of my trainers, wearing hand-me-downs that Dad has got from jumble sales or charity shops. I wear the same trousers for three or four years so the bottoms end up halfway up my shins. Most people are like that and I don't feel like I stick out. In any case I don't really care what other people think. When you're getting what I'm getting at home that's the last thing on your mind.

Besides, I love school. I try to have as much fun as I can when I'm at school. I walk through the school gates thinking 'joy' and enter into a different, safer world where the nightmare of the previous night's beating can seem like a lifetime ago – something that happened on another planet and not even to me but to my twin brother – and unfortunately that affects my performance at school because everything that goes on within the school gates is sheer light relief as far as I'm concerned. There's nothing they could possibly do or say that would have been able to control me, or would put fear into me in comparison with what happens at home.

I've got a picture of myself in a little white shirt and striped red school tie – not my normal clothes I wear for school but they look good in the photo. I've just started school and I'm grinning from ear to ear. I've got this Edward Scissorhands pudding-bowl haircut – my hair's light brown and matted – and my face is a little red. That's partly because of freckles and partly because it's still swollen from a beating Dad gave me a couple of nights before. I've got styes in both eyes and a cold sore on my mouth, and if you look closely you'll see my eyes aren't as happy as my grin would make you think.

When I'm at school and free of my jailer I put up a front to protect myself, so no one knows what's happening at home. I clown it up and it's like that Miracles song Dad sometimes plays and sings along to, 'Tears of a Clown'. The only good thing I've got from Dad is that he can be very funny, and so can I. Dad loves playing tricks. He'll brick up someone's front door, or get his next-door neighbour's washing, put brown sauce on it and put it back on their washing line, and I do similar things at school – when I manage to get there – like moving people's chairs away before they sit down. Or when we're in the canteen eating school dinner, I'll unscrew the top of the salt cellar and leave it loose on top, so when someone sprinkles salt on their chips, it all falls out.

Dad's been taking me to the pub from the age of five. If I go off to the toilet, by the time I've come back there'll be a group of men surrounding him and he's entertaining them all, telling them stories and laughing, the centre of attention. But he's lousy at listening to other people. He'll make a joke out of everything they say, even if it's a serious conversation.

Having Dad's sense of humour helps me right through my school years. Even in my first years at school, I get by with quips and practical jokes. Besides, just getting out of the house and away from Dad makes school a holiday. School's a breeze for me – it's a lark. I'm aided and abetted in this by my best friend Calum, who makes my time at school – when I do go to school, that is – about the only thing that makes life worth living for me.

Calum Patterson! A kid in exactly the same boat as me but it's his mum who's bringing him up alone and using Calum as a punch bag. We never really speak about our home life, but we just know even at a young age what each of us is going through. Calum is a short-arse like me. He's a right Scottish-looking child, with a ginger bowl-cut hairdo and freckles, and even though he's just a kid he has a boxer's nose and bags under his eyes like me. Like me he wears Staypress trousers, and British Home Stores jumper and shirt from the social grant that all people on the dole receive. His tie is always wrapped around his head. When *Karate Kid* comes out Calum thinks that's him, running past people screaming high-pitched noises like *hiiiyyaa*.

We both walk around school with ripped trousers and scuffed shoes from climbing up the drainpipe onto the school roof. If anyone kicks a ball up there, we're the monkeys that will go and get it – well, we're the only two daft and fearless enough for the job. Calum is a lot like me. The way that he always cracks jokes or makes up names for people by using their most noticeable features.

For instance, we call ginger Garry Copper Crutch; fat Paul is Rollo; Alec with the glasses is Specky Ecky; and Peter Humphrey is Bogey, after Humphrey Bogart. Compared with what we both go through at home, our lives in school are fantastic, brilliant – a world away from the torture dens we have to go back to at 3.30 p.m. It is somewhere we can be ourselves, without the pressure of watching every word we say in case we're mauled.

One day Calum and I are walking along the corridor between classes when we see a girl from the year above us arguing with a boy about how good looking she is. I only catch the end of the conversation. 'I'm nicer looking than your lass, she's a pure minger.'

As we walk past, she turns to us. 'Lads, do you think I'm fit, couldn't I be a film star?'

'No, love,' Calum replies, quick as a flash, 'you've definitely got a face for radio.'

Her face turns purple and she proceeds to chase us down the corridor for the next two minutes so we're late for the next class.

He has so many one-liners. Like the one he deals out to Claire Clark, a lovely, big girl, who's always taking the mick out of me and Calum. Claire's got a really pretty face but she's a little overweight. She's told everyone in school that Calum dresses up in his mum's clothes at the weekend and the whole school has been slagging him off for days, so Calum makes up a rumour that Claire has been hit by a taxi and when the police came, they asked the taxi driver why he hit her. The taxi man replied, 'I never had enough petrol to go around her!'

He tells this joke in front of about fifty people and I take to my heels before he has a chance to finish, as I know what's coming. It is hilarious and Claire sees the funny side of it after we both get out of hospital.

I'm joking; we couldn't offend Claire if we tried, as we're like the Three Musketeers. She wouldn't let anyone else talk to her like that, but with Calum and me it's different. In school the three of us hang around together except when football is being played at lunchtime. She goes with the girls – skipping or swapping photos of Boy George or Duran Duran, or whatever it is they do. Claire's mum and dad split up when she was young and her mum was an alcoholic like my dad. But Claire's mum never beats her – she just doesn't bother to look after her. It's called neglect. I'm not saying that's not as bad as what happened to me and Calum – it's just a different kind of abuse.

At school it's an amazing adventure just walking from one class to another, people tripping each other up and hitting each other with water balloons, but it's not like at home –

there's never any violence. In class we play pranks on each other. The one I like best is tying people's rucksacks to those all-in-one tables and chairs. They're made out of metal and wood, and the chair and desk are welded together so that if you tie someone's bag straps around the metal bar when they have their backpack on, they'll stand up and end up in a heap on the floor, entangled in the furniture. I don't know why I find it so funny or even why I do it, but that's my party piece. Everyone has their own, and that's mine.

One of the effects of the nightly torture sessions – the beatings and interrogations that go on into the early hours of the morning – is that I fall asleep a lot when I'm at school. I don't pay attention – it's not important to me compared with what's going on at home, and as the teachers are quite strict I often get into trouble. I'm always messing around. But I have to be careful at school not to cross the line – if I get expelled or excluded I'll be in for it at home.

As for my bruises, a couple of teachers do ask, 'What happened to yir face?'

'Oh, I was playing on the monkey bars and fell off.'

I'm a great liar as Dad has taught me to lie. I've become an expert through having to tell stories to the debt collectors and anyone else who comes to the door.

'Just get rid of them,' Dad would say.

I'm never bulled at school and I never bully anyone else either. I hate bullies as that's what my dad is, and any kind of bullying behaviour makes me see red. I do play practical jokes on other kids though.

It can be quite dangerous messing about in school, as there's a fine line between getting the cane or belt from a teacher and Dad being called in. I had to learn very quickly what I could get away with and what's over the line. When Dad's been called up to the school, it always ends in near death experiences, so when the headmaster calls him up on this occasion I'm not looking forward to it one bit.

I have been arguing with the Janitor constantly about who's best – Dundee United or Dundee. Obviously it's Dundee United but the Janny is a Dundee fan and can't handle the fact that a seven year old knows so much about football and I don't think it helps that the headmaster walks past and hears me tell him, 'Dundee have never won anything, they are shite.'

That's only one of the words I've picked up from Dad over the last few years. I go home that day expecting to be kicked around the house for the next few hours. Sitting in my room getting changed out of my school clothes I think, he's just told the headmaster he will deal with me at home, I'm in for it now!

But a calm voice comes from the living room. 'Charlie, can yi come through here, son?'

That doesn't sound like the normal tone. *What's going on?* I'm feeling very confused as I walk down the Hall of Imminent Death, the dark corridor that leads to the living room. I often think of it as my long walk of fear to the execution chamber, at the end of which is the Electric Chair. That's the chair I have to sit on in the living room while Dad interrogates me for hour after hour until I can't think any more and I feel like I'm going mad. I call it the Electric Chair because after four or five hours of questioning my head often feels like it has been fried.

'Don't worry aboot what happened the day.'

Wait a minute! I think, *where's the camera?* Surely Jeremy Beadle's going to jump out in a minute and then they'll both kick the shit out of me.

'That blue nose cunt disnay hey a clue, never let dickheads like that tell yi that Dundee are better than United, but if I ever catch you swearing like that again I'll rattle yir arse!'

I'm standing in front of him waiting for the punchline, then the punch, but nothing happens. I think it must be another one of his mind games to see if I'll bite but I get off scot-free. *YEEHAA!*

Brilliant! I think, if I ever get in trouble again, I'll tell Dad that they've been slagging off Dundee United and I've had to defend them. Then he'll fly downstairs in his steel toecap boots, and kick lumps out of anybody who says a wrong word.

What a strange, strange man. He doesn't even tell me off, let alone batter or torture me. Maybe he's been smoking something funny and has forgotten what I actually did. Or maybe the sicko just loves Dundee United that much. As he's always telling me, my grandfather used to play for them and Dad could have signed too, but he passed up on the offer because he didn't want any help from my granddad to become a professional footballer. I suspect it was more down to the fact that he was too violent on the pitch. I believe he went for trials with Norwich and some other English clubs but his temper always got the better of him, and managers don't like smart arses with bad attitudes.

Whatever the reason for his leniency, I'm off the hook for today. I have to count myself lucky, but then again, whoever deals out the lucky cards seems to be ignoring me most days of my childhood.

There are a few exceptions, though; I do have the occasional good times with Dad and with my family, which shine out like a beacon in the darkness of my miserable childhood.

Chapter Seven

The Laughter that Hurts

At Christmas I'll get a few presents, like a tracksuit or a football. If Dad has a girlfriend we go to hers for dinner. But some Christmases I've been battered so badly the night before that when I wake up in the morning I've found that Dad has torn the wrapping paper and the presents to shreds.

This doesn't just happen once but on two or three occasions and each time I'm devastated. From all the excitement of Christmas Eve, peeping at the presents sitting under the plastic tree glowing with little red, yellow and blue lights, I haven't been able to believe my eyes the next morning to find them hacked to bits. I often wonder if he does it deliberately so that he can watch the expression on my face change from the joy of anticipation to misery and disappointment.

And to add to my ever-growing confusion, I can never predict from one Christmas morning to the next whether I will find him crying and penitent, trying to put them back together again, or whether he will be sitting amongst the torn wrapping paper with a glass of vodka in his hand, waiting patiently to see the look on my face so that he can really twist the Xmas knife.

There's only one really good Christmas and that's when I'm seven. Dad says to me, 'I'll gi' yi thirty-quid for clothes or I'll get yi a bike, which is it?'

I'd love a bike but the thought of all that money for clothes, or anything else, is just too tempting so I pick clothes. By Christmas Eve I've picked the clothes I want – a light blue tracksuit from the Barnardo's charity shop in Reform Street – and even have a bit of cash left over to spend on Mars bars and comics.

My favourite comic is the *Dandy* because it's got Desperate Dan. My mouth always waters looking at his favourite food, cow pies. I also like football sticker albums, and will stand at the local shop swapping stickers with other kids trying to fill the book. So I buy a *Beano* and *Dandy* and a sticker album and *The Observers Book of Wild Animals* which I get from Barnardo's for a pound. I love any wildlife books and I'm in love with white tigers even though I've never seen a real one.

On Christmas morning Dad gets me up. 'Go and make me a cup of tea,' he says.

I go into the kitchen and I can't believe my eyes – there's a brand new shiny red Raleigh bike – he's got me both! And what's more, we get through the day without him giving me a beating.

The longest I go without a beating is two days so the next day, Boxing Day, when I go out and play football and get grass on my new clothes he's back on form, battering and torturing me for hours, asking me questions – sometimes the same one – over and over again.

And another thing: he confiscates the bike. I even think he only gave me it so he could take it away again. Once again I feel torn up, like those bits of wrapping paper he's shredded. I'm shaking with fury and frustration yet I can't show it to him so I go out and kick trees and lampposts, or if I'm playing football I smash the ball at anyone I'm playing with so hard they stare at me in surprise, but I don't care. A few days later I get the bike back though. That's when he's feeling guilty the morning after he's given me another battering.

The mental torture is always worse, I can take the physical punishment – he can smash a baseball bat over my head and it won't hurt as much as if he's got me in a corner, mentally torturing me. It's hard to explain this except to say that bruises and cuts can heal, and it's sometimes hard even to remember what the physical pain felt like a few days later when I'm at school. But the constant questions are like a corkscrew into my brain and my mind and my soul. They haunt me for days, weeks, sometimes months and even years, and I will hear his voice in my sleep, I can never seem to escape it. And then there's the fear and frustration of not knowing what's the best thing to do or say, to find the words that will make him stop, or at least not say something that will make him spin out the questioning for hour after hour.

I think Dad should have joined the army as he would have been the most persistent interrogation officer on the planet. One night with him and even Shergar would have come out of hiding, handed himself in, given himself up. OK, Jock, he'd say. You win. It's like you said, I just did it for the publicity.

Once a year on New Year's Eve, which is Hogmanay, my Gran and Granddad, Dad's parents, have a family get-together at their house.

They live in Hilltown in Dundee in a semi-detached three-bedroom council house. Gran is small, with dark permed hair and very smooth clear skin; she's always cooking in the kitchen and calling all her grandchildren the wrong name.

Granddad is quite reserved. He has funny one-liners but doesn't really say much. He goes to the pub and plays dominos and bets on the horses. He has dark hair and dark skin, and is bow-legged from his football days. Nowadays he's only five foot three.

All my uncles and aunts on my dad's side come to these get-togethers – Dad's three sisters and their husbands; his brother Danny with his girlfriend; and me and my eight cousins (six boys and two girls). The parties start at seven and go on until midnight, though occasionally they last until four or five in the morning.

We watch *Scotch and Wry* on telly – it's a comedy sketch show with characters like Supercop, a bungling traffic police-man who stops cars that turn out to be driven by people like Batman. But the character I like best is this minister who has his water spiked with gin just before he starts giving a ser-mon and then gets completely drunk. It really makes me laugh, but it's a funny kind of laughter as it hurts, probably because it makes me think of Dad – and that makes it even funnier and more painful at the same time.

After that's over we count down the bells to Hogmanay. As the clock hits twelve Scottish music comes blasting out of the speakers and everyone bursts into their rendition of the Highland Fling: 'Da da da da da da da, di di di di di di di, na na na na na na na'. All us kids will be firing party poppers at each other in the kitchen.

The grown-ups'll be singing Scottish songs, like 'Flower of Scotland' and 'Scotland the Brave', or 'Mull of Kintyre', or 'Donald Where's Your Troosers?' Then of course we all link arms and sing 'Auld Lang Syne' and eat Scottish shortbread and dance, jiving to rock 'n' roll and knocking everything over. The girls, my cousins, will be doing their own dance routines, and all the adults get drunk.

Dad tries not to overstep the mark in front of the rest of the family at Gran's house. He's lippy but not nasty. But although he always starts the evening on his best behaviour, he'll end up fighting with Uncle Grant, who's a Protestant and a Mason. Dad hates Protestants nearly as much as he hates Masons.

Then someone will say, 'Where's Gran?' and then we'll wander around looking for her, although everyone knows where she is. She's hiding in the airing cupboard, drunk every year, and we'll find her sleeping in there after a few sherries.

We kill ourselves with laughter but when I think about it I realise that she probably hides in that cupboard a lot – she could even be doing it every night as she may be hiding from Granddad. Dad was the oldest of all his siblings. He's told me that Granddad used to beat him and Gran up, and I've heard this from other members of the family. I'm fond of Granddad and don't want to believe he could beat up Gran or Dad in the same way Dad beats me up, but that's what Dad tells me.

I've also heard that Granddad used to take the fuse out of the electricity box so that Gran didn't have any heating or light and then he'd lock Gran in all night and leave her without electricity while he went out to the pub. I find it almost impossible to believe, but he might be as clever and cunning as Dad.

There's a small bar in the corner that Granddad will sit behind, ringing a gold bell and shouting 'Last orders!' every time he serves a drink. He'll hit me on the back of the head with some peanuts and then look away smiling as if it isn't him. I think it's funny but it does make me wonder.

Sometimes when Dad's drunk he'll go on about how Granddad would take him out into the woods away from the rest of his family and then beat him up – but he also beat him up in the house as well – and finally threw Dad out of the house when he was twelve. Dad had to scavenge for food – he's never tired of telling me that.

I suppose Dad may say this to make me think it's normal – what he does to me – and when he's sometimes very drunk and self-pitying, even to feel sorry for him. But although of course I have no way of judging whether it's normal or not, there's no way I'm going to feel sorry for him when he's battering and torturing me every other night. But that doesn't stop him from dishing out his hard luck story.

'Yir grandfather, yi think he's the bee's knees, don't yi, but yi don't know what it was like. Yi've got an easy life. Yi've got a roof over your head.'

I think, yeah I wish I was out of the house at twelve.

But even so, I always get on well with Granddad. He tells me stories about when he played for Dundee United and I really look up to him.

Dad had a chance to go with Dundee United too, but because he was stubborn he said he didn't want any help from my grandfather and didn't want to be known as getting a game with the club because of his father, so at one point he went to England and had trials for a few English clubs. He tells me he even played some reserve matches for West Brom, but I don't know what to believe any more as my brain is controlled by his way of thinking.

Gran was a professional dancer in the Pally in Dundee years ago. She was Irish and Granddad met her in Ireland when he was playing football for Glentoran Football Club in East Belfast in the 1950s. Granddad was a Glaswegian. Then later he signed for United. After he had finished as a professional footballer he worked as a hospital porter but he was still involved in Dundee United, and the players used to come to his house for dinner sometimes – John Clark, Kevin Gallacher and many more.

As Dad now manages the Dundee West Under-14s football team, we go up to Glenshee in the mountains every year with my cousin Shane and stay at the Spittal of Glenshee Hotel. Shane is six months younger than me and absolutely bonkers and hilarious at the same time. He has the kind of personality that means he has to say exactly what's on his mind – he can't hold things in for more than ten seconds at a time, and his laugh is infectious. When he starts, everyone does too. Such a likeable person.

There's loads to do apart from playing football – hillwalking, golfing, horseriding, shooting, mountain biking and even hang-gliding, but Shane and I just enjoy larking around.

There's also this little goalkeeper in our team called Willy. He wears old, worn but ironed pyjamas with creases in them and National Health glasses with Sellotape in the middle –

he's a right little geek and he's useless in goal into the bargain. He must have let in about 15 goals a game – he's a crap goalie, but at the same time a dead nice wee lad. A bit like Walter the Softie out of the *Beano* but harmless. In any case Dad doesn't care how good his team is, he's more interested in where they live as he has to pick them up or drop them off after a game.

I'm seven on this particular occasion when we go to Glenshee and the news has filtered out of the radio on the way up here that there's a murderer loose in the mountains who has been going around killing people. It must be about half nine at night and there's a man sitting at the bar with a mack on and a big handlebar moustache and hat, and Shane and I whisper to Willy 'That's that murderer!'

Willy's shitting himself. 'No, it's not?' he says, alarmed.

'Yeah, that's him. We've just seen his picture on the news.'

Another guy sitting near us hears what we're saying and knows we're winding Willy up, and says, 'Cut it out, lads.'

But we ignore him and go on saying to Willy, 'No, seriously, that guy – he's definitely the murderer. Look at that moustache. I'll bet he's got an axe under that coat!'

Just then the guy turns and looks at us and takes off out of the front door of bar. Even though I know it isn't him, the man scares me. He couldn't have timed it any better as he stares back towards us as he leaves.

Meanwhile Willy's in a blue funk. He tears off petrified in his PJs, while the barman looks on in shock at this skinny little ankle-biter whizzing past him like a skeleton on Pro-Plus. Willy's eyes are even bigger than normal as a combination of pure blind panic and his thick milk-bottle glasses make him look completely demented.

The bunkhouse we're all sleeping in has a room on each side of a corridor with bunk beds in every room, so Willy crawls in there with sheets over him as he's now terrified. But we crawl along the floor in the dark towards his bed saying, 'The murderer's gonna get you! The murderer's gonna get you!'

Shane's one of those people who after you stop he'll keep it going. He wound up this little lad Willy for hours and hours. Maybe it's something in the family genes. Shane just enjoys spinning out a joke, while Dad enjoys spinning out the torture.

Anyway, Willy's in his bunk bed and Shane goes up and sticks a football sock over his arm and puts it over the top bunk of the bed and grabs Willy's mouth with it.

'Ahhhhhhhhhh!' Willy screams. He's only wearing his Y-fronts and terry towelling socks, and he goes sprinting through the corridor past a shocked barman for a second time.

'*There's a murderer! Phone the police!*' Willy screams frantically at the women in reception. '*He's in my room. Phone the police!*'

At that moment we stumble in after him, laughing our heads off, and give Willy the good news – it wasn't the murderer after all but his twin brother. Willy stares from one to the other of us in disbelief and then finally realises we've been winding him up all along.

The next day, we go mountain climbing – well, it's really hillwalking as given the size of us anything bigger than a molehill looks like a mountain. They always have to entice Shane to climb up the mountains because he's overweight, and I won't say no to a bit of enticement myself, so they bribe us with Mars bars. But me and Shane end up getting lost and bored after the box of Mars bars runs out, so we try to take a short cut back to the hotel. They have the mountain rescue team out searching for us for six hours and when they get back we're playing pool in the poolroom.

Of course I end up getting battered for it. Shane's fine though; he only gets a mouthful from Dad, but if you shout at Shane he just looks at you as though you're daft, so there isn't much point.

Chapter Eight

Twenty Pound Note

You can only compare Dundee in November to the Arctic or maybe Siberia – the wind is enough to take you off your feet as Dundee is built on a hill (the Law Hill). It rains ten months of the year and snows five months – yes, you do get them both together.

Dundee is made up of around fifteen different areas called schemes, and every scheme has a gang, each of which is known by a set of initials – you have YMB (Young Mary Boys), YKH (Young Kirkton Huns), YLF (Young Lochee Fleet), YHH (Young Hilltown Huns), FS (Fintry Shams), WS (Whitfield Shams), AP (Ardler Pirates) and many, many more. At the back of Dundee is St Mary's and Kirkton leading on to the bottom of the Sidlaw Hills. It's probably one of the most picturesque places, leading up to Coupar Angus, Dunkeld, Clunie Loch and the rest of

Perthshire – all up to the mountains that spread across the north of Scotland.

It's a beautiful place, but throughout my childhood in the 1980s all I seem to be aware of is the pain, misery, violence and drink-fuelled torture that are rife around me. Every third kid I know is part of a single-parent family who are being abused or neglected by their parents, keepers or guardians and no one bats an eyelid about what's really going on.

It's November 1983 and a really bad winter has started early. The roads are covered in snow and ice and it's freezing. We have mastered a fast way of getting to the shops from the Closies or tenements. It takes about five minutes to walk there, but in the winter we wait for the cars coming round the corner to hitch a ride. It gets dark really early as well, so no one can see us kids hiding behind the hedge. We'll wait until the cars slow down as they turn the corner, then run out and grab onto the bumpers and hitch a free slide in a sitting position down to the local shops, then let go and slide for about twenty yards until it stops.

On this particular night, Dad has asked me to go to the shops and get him some fags and milk. He hands me a twenty pound note and tells me to hurry back.

'*And don't piss around wi yir daft mates – come right back.*'

So I set off on my mission – every time I do something for Dad it's a mission, not an errand. When I get outside all the lads – my gang, shall we say – are all out chucking snowballs at each other and waiting for cars to come around the corner so they can take a trip on them.

Stevie G is a year younger than me. He's a bit of a snot nose kid but he's always up for anything – you can tell him to do something and he'll do it, no questions. He's the first one I see when I come out the close and I ask him if he can come to the shops with me and hang on a bumper. He jumps at the chance and we both take off on my mission – it's a bit like a James Bond mission – which has now become his mission, to return with the goods. We get to the shops, get the things my dad wants, and head back homewards, Mission Accomplished, with the goods in the bag, looking for a car to hang onto.

We hang onto a car going up towards the tenements, but it speeds up a bit too fast and I'm finding it hard to hang on and when we fly past the tenement I have to let go or who knows where I might end up. Then Stevie follows suit and we both roll about twenty yards up the road like a couple of bundles of tumbleweed. Luckily neither of us are injured so we brush all the snow off and head back down to the close, laughing about our close encounter.

I tell Stevie I'll be back in five minutes, as I have to give Dad his things – oh yeah and thank God I never burst the milk or that would really be a disaster. I run upstairs to the front door, open it and take the long, slow walk up the hall and into the living room where Dad's watching football.

'Did yi get the fags and milk?'

'Yep,' I say, all proud of myself. 'There you go, Dad.'

'Put the milk in the fridge and stick the kettle on, will yi.'

'Alright, Dad.' I run into the kitchen and boil the kettle, make a cup of tea and take it to him. 'There you go, Dad. Can I go back out to play now?'

'Yeah, on you go.' He looks up at me. 'Just one more thing, have yi put the change on the kitchen table?'

My heart goes *bang*. Wait a minute. I am frantically searching my pockets for the £17 change. I had it in my hand when I came out the shop and after that I grabbed the car bumper and then fell off the car up the road.

Oh shit! I think to myself. *Where's the fucking change?*

'Yi better be fucking joking,' Dad's saying. He can tell by my face that something's up.

'I think it's in the kitchen, Dad.'

Oh please God, please be in the kitchen.

He stands up out of his chair. The sweat is running down the sides of my head; my heart is pumping, my palms are sticky with sweat, and I'm saying ten Please Gods a second in my head.

'Yi think it's in the kitchen?' he says in a weird crying, angry, shouty voice. It's probably the scariest voice I have ever heard. 'Yi better pray it's in the fucking kitchen. Get out this hoose and find it, and don't come back in until yi do. That was my last twenty pounds, yi fucking half wit.'

So I run to the kitchen – *nothing*.

I shoot out of the door and down to the road where I fell off the car. It's now suddenly turned into Mission Impossible. All the kids in the area help me search frantically for this money, from the tenements to the shops, covering every lump of snow on the way. But it's gone forever and so am I. I try to walk as slow as a snail back home because I know what's coming – well, I think I do, as Dad will always change what he does to screw with my mind. He'll play these mind games and try to confuse me.

I walk into the house and shuffle slowly up the hall towards the living room and push the door open, praying that he's found it on the side or something. I think he knows I have lost it by the way I come in. He's sitting on the windowsill obviously watching me turning over every lump of snow and ice from the window.

'Sit on the couch,' he says.

I walk over and sit down.

'What did I tell yi before you went to the shops?' Staring at me with those big beady eyes.

'You told me to stay away from my mates and hurry back with your fags.'

'Correct, now did I tell yi to lose my last twenty pounds – yi fucking moron?' He is talking in a calm voice that I have never heard before. Usually he'll get drunk and then start on me for not doing dishes or for being two or three minutes late home from school and beat me up for a few hours or spit in my face, but this is a new one. I have never seen this before. It's like *Question Time* with insults.

71

'Are yi retarded or did yi do that deliberate to push my buttons?'

I don't know what to say. If I say no, then he'll reply, 'What no, yi're not retarded or no yi didn't do it deliberate?' Then if I say 'No to both, Dad,' he'll come back with '*Fuck yi*. Are yi a retard or did yi do it deliberate?'

I'm gonna have to answer this or I'm dead.

'I'm a retard, Dad.'

'Yir my son, so yi must be calling me a retard – is that what yir saying?'

'No Dad, I did it deliberate.'

'What did yi dae it deliberate fir, Charlie?'

'No I mean, I didn't do it deliberate but—'

'Well, which is it? Are yi tryin' to be clever wi' me?'

'No, Dad—'

'So yi're sayin' I'm stupid, is that it?'

I try to think what I've just said. *Did I call him stupid?* I can't think.

'So now yi canna even be bothered ti gee' me an answer, eh?'

'No, Dad, I'm not trying to be clever with you.'

'You're naturally stupid, like yi think I am – is that what yir sayin?'

Well, this goes on for hours. To say I am confused doesn't begin to describe it. Imagine some young kid who hasn't slept for three nights is brought into a police interrogation room and then subjected to hours of questioning about a murder he hasn't committed. By the end he'll be begging to sign the confession statement. That's me. I'm that kid. Imagine a hard-boiled police officer who no longer cares whether he gets a result or not as he simply gets a buzz out of inflicting mental torture for its own sake. That's my dad.

So in the end I start crying and ask if he can please just hit me because I don't know what else to say. I'm falling asleep with the questions, as they're so confusing.

'Oh, so you decide your punishment, do ya? OK yi fucking little cunt, yi lose my last few bob and you decide what yir gonna get.'

He walks over and sits beside me on the couch while taking a swig of a vodka and Coke, then he puts it down on the table.

'Give me yir hand.'

'Why, Dad, what for?'

'Give me yir hand,' he says in a calm voice.

So I put my hand out towards him reluctantly. He takes a vicelike grip of my wrist and pulls it towards him and sinks his teeth deep into my fingers.

Ahhhh! They start bleeding and I scream at the top of my lungs.

'Please Dad, let go.' His fanglike teeth are now piercing through the skin below my knuckles as he makes a loud, growling, angry noise, shaking his head from side to side like a pitbull with a doll in its mouth. He then lays his thirteen-stone body on me, covers my mouth and starts biting different parts of my body from head to toe. I can feel his teeth piercing through my trousers and skin, and can feel the warm blood trickling out of all the areas he has bitten. At one point I think I try to bite his hand to get some air as I can't breathe – and that makes him ten times worse.

This goes on for about forty minutes. I am trying to scream but he's too strong, and with the smell of vodka and smoke now blowing in my face, I'm beginning to feel sick. It's like being attacked by a pack of wolves. My face has been bitten, so have my arms, legs, chest, back and hands.

He finally gets off me and calmly picks up the salt and vinegar from the coffee table beside his bottle of vodka and pours it over the bite marks he has made all over me.

The pain is unbelievable. He is now standing over me, emptying the salt all over my face. He doesn't say a word as I try to block the salt from hitting the hole in my face. Then the worst words I have ever heard come spilling out of his mouth.

'Maybe I'll just have ti eat yi since I've got *fuck all in the cupboards!* Yi little bastard!'

I'm lying there praying for God to give me a heart attack or let me die quickly before he eats me. I have never been so scared in my life. So much so that I think God must have heard me because for some reason Dad suddenly stops – he changes so quickly it's like someone has taken over his body. He sits back in his chair and has another drink of vodka and just leaves me lying on the couch for a few hours, until he falls asleep.

Something has changed tonight as well. This night is the point in my life when I stop caring about anyone. My trust in the world has gone and if anyone ever touches me from now on, they'll have to suffer the consequences that follow. When he can tell me he loves me one moment (usually when he's sober in the morning, when he's seen what a mess he made of me the night before) and then do exactly the same thing to me the following night after a few vodkas, it's enough to make me never trust another human being again.

Occasionally after he's beaten me up really badly he'll stop drinking for a day or two – maybe out of remorse – but the sober periods don't ever last long. He can't handle not drinking. He can't handle me looking at him like that when my face is still a mess and he soon falls off the wagon again.

There are just a few times when he's really hammered when he'll give me a genuine hug of affection, but then he's just as likely to follow it up by slamming me across the room.

And all the while the beatings keep coming. For years to come I take many more of them, with broken ribs, a fractured skull, black eyes, and mental torture, sometimes for ten hours at a time. I spend most of my childhood years stuck with a drunken, sadistic sociopath with little regard for human life.

I don't know if you have ever been stuck in a situation with someone on your own. It's just you and them in your own world, with them controlling every word you say and every move you make. I can only compare my childhood to being held captive in a concentration camp or torture chamber. The beatings I receive are not just a couple of punches or kicks. They are sometimes twelve-hour interrogation sessions, with nipping, biting, poking in the eyes, and pulling clumps of hair from my head.

Sometimes Dad will actually be laughing at me as I'm flinching and this can go on for a couple of hours. At times like this, my mind tends to drift off to other places. Even though my body is still there my head is somewhere completely different. That's how I think I deal with it. It simply doesn't occur to me that what is going on in my life is highly abnormal. I even assume that it's like this for everyone – that children the whole world over experience the same kind of sustained torture that I go through day after day.

I don't understand why the neighbours never do anything, as when he beats me up marble ashtrays get smashed through the front window, and once he even throws a TV at me and it lands in the street. Between the ages of five and seven I'm beaten virtually every night – and after that every two or three nights – but the beatings get more ferocious. And when his girlfriends are there we get half each.

On one occasion he pours bleach on me; another time he tells me to drink it. I just hold the bottle to my mouth without drinking it and when he takes a gulp of his vodka I just throw the bleach bottle on the floor behind him. He's that drunk he doesn't even notice.

Another time, after he has kicked me into a corner, he rolls me up in the rug and then rolls it towards him and sits with his feet on it; he ends up watching TV with me trapped in the rug.

'This is comfy,' he says, looking down at me.

On yet another occasion I am strangled so hard that I pass out and he bursts my eardrum. When I come round he says, 'You're a good little actor, I'll give you that, the shaking on the floor looked quite real.'

At that stage I have obviously had a fit through lack of air. But from this particular night, when I genuinely believe that he is going to eat me – devour his own son like a cannibal – I begin biding my time, waiting for the day when I am the same size as him.

This is the night that my pain turns to hate.

Chapter Nine

A Boy's Best Friend

One reason my childhood is so strange is that Dad is a totally different man when he's sober. That's what's so confusing about being a kid in my house. He'll take me camping and fishing, and to football matches to Tannadice Stadium to watch Dundee United.

He stands at the segregation fence between both sets of supporters and shouts abuse at them. I sit down on the wall next to the pitch eating a Wallace's pie and drinking hot Bovril, watching and listening to our supporters behind one of the goals, in an area called the Shed. I always want to go in there and bounce around and sing, but I'm too small.

The atmosphere is brilliant, fantastic. The most popular song is 'Let's All Do the Shed Boys' Dance – na na na na – na na na!' then everyone behind the goal goes crazy, like they're in a moshpit.

At one game Dad is having an argument with a stranger in the crowd about how crap Iain Ferguson is. He's heckling the player the whole game until Ferguson smashes the ball in from forty yards out. It's one of the best goals I've ever seen.

The stranger turns to Dad with a smile on his face.

'What about that, mate?'

Dad looks him in the eye, trying not to laugh and says, 'That was his attempt at a back pass!'

Then we move to another area of the ground with Dad laughing away to himself.

If Dundee United win, we go to the pub. I walk through all the bodies with my Coke, waist high to everyone else. I can't see anything but I love the singing and the atmosphere – I don't even mind the cigarette smoke which is sometimes stifling.

If they lose we go to the off-licence, which is called Party Time, for vodka and Coke, and then go home. At times like this I have to be particularly on my guard, watching Dad like a hawk, waiting on him to change, because I know I'm going to get it.

As well as camping, fishing and football, Dad also gets me the best friend I have ever had in my life: her name is Bonnie, she's six weeks old and she's a longhaired Alsatian puppy, jet black. At this time in my life, at the age of eight, she's the best thing that has ever happened to me. I've had a dog before, called Lucky, but he got run over by a car – a bit ironic that I gave him that name really, as he clearly wasn't that lucky! Oh yeah, and I had had a hamster but my next-door neighbour tried to see if it could fly by throwing it out of the bedroom window.

You learn a lot about animals when you're young. I've learnt that dogs are softer than cars and hamsters definitely cannot fly.

Bonnie, my soulmate, my Alsatian, will follow me wherever I go. I can't even go to the toilet, as she will sit outside the door and wait on me coming out. I've had her from six weeks old and we're mad about each other. She is my best friend, someone or something I can trust one hundred per cent, no question. She will never bite me and I will never leave the house without her.

When Bonnie first comes into my life as a puppy, she is obviously not house-trained and has never before seen this new world that she has quickly become a part of. So my first job is to bring her up and teach her how to go outside for the loo and not bite anyone, except Dad! I put newspaper down in the kitchen, as she hasn't had her needles yet, so she can't go outside for the loo. She is a really clever dog – as most Alsatians are – but she is different, more like a human. The way she acts and the way she understands every word I say.

One morning when she is about three months old, I've woken up at 7.30 a.m. for school and Dad has been up all night, on the piss again. Bonnie is lying on the bed across my feet – she isn't allowed on the bed but as soon as everyone is sleeping she has the run of the house. I love waking up next to her in the morning – it's like having a pal that never argues with you or judges things that you do. Bonnie sees that I have woken up and comes bounding up to the top of the bed, licking my face and sticking her head under the covers, so that I will pull them back and let her in.

But I can sense there's something wrong. It's like she knows that she has done something she shouldn't and she's come to me for protection. I can hear Dad getting up, yawning, then the living-room door opening. Then all of a sudden …

'Oh you dirty bastard! Charlie, where's that fucking mutt?'

I try to pull the cover over Bonnie's head but she is as stiff as a board and shaking like a leaf.

'Charlie, I'll not ask you again. That cunt has shit all over the lobby and I've just stood in it.'

Dad falls asleep in a pair of shorts every night in front of the two-bar electric council-issued fire, so I know he never has any socks on. I imagine Bonnie's shit squelching through his toes and it makes me feel sick – not just out of nausea but also anxiety about how he will react – but it also makes me laugh inside at the same time. I think I'm laughing because of nerves and because one of us is about to become a sparring partner. I just hope he'll take it out on me and not on Bonnie.

The bedroom door opens and a big dark figure stands filling the doorway. 'Bonnie, come here!'

81

She doesn't move; she just pushes her head into my chest with her ears pointing backwards, shaking with fear.

'Bonnie here!'

'Dad, I'll clean it.'

'Shut yir fucking mouth or I'll rub yir nose in it.'

Bonnie still hasn't moved, so he walks across towards my bed and puts his hand under the covers and grabs her by the tail, dragging her out of my bed.

Her claws are desperately trying to hang onto the piss-stained bed sheets as she yelps at me, looking for me to pull her back in. I just freeze as he drags her out of the room and closes the door. I want to help her but my body has frozen and isn't listening to my head.

Help her, yi coward, I keep saying to myself.

I jump up out of bed and put my ear against the door. I can hear Bonnie screaming like a baby that needs feeding and Dad's voice, very sharp and fast, saying things like, 'Do yi like the taste of yir own shit, do yi! Go on eat it yi bastard, fuckin' eat it.'

I feel like busting out of the door and rubbing his face in the shit, the cruel bastard, and I'm now looking around the room wondering what I can hit him with to stop him hitting my friend, my sister from a different species.

The noise suddenly stops so I run back into bed and jump under the covers. The door opens and then closes again after Bonnie has been thrown back into the room, covered in her own shit. She jumps up on my bed and scrambles under the covers beside me, covering me in it as well, but I don't care as she is shaking like a leaf and I have to protect her. The door opens again and I think, here we go, it's my turn now.

Dad walks over to the bed and tips it upside down, so that Bonnie and I both fall onto the floor, and I try to drag the mattress on top of us both so he can't get a clear shot. The door closes again and I can hear the floorboards in the hall creak as he walks back towards the living room. You could hear a pin drop, if it wasn't for Bonnie moaning and her teeth chattering together.

The smell is horrible as I have landed on top of her in a kind of spoon position, and all the shit he has rubbed on her is wafting in my face, but I don't dare move as I think we're both safe under there. Bonnie never budges either; it's like she's thinking exactly the same as me.

We must have lain there for about three and a half hours and Bonnie has now calmed down and is trying to lick my face.

'Stop it, girl,' I say in a calm voice. 'Cut it out.'

She is getting more playful as the ordeal recedes and when I smile and laugh at her, that's her cue to start hamming it up. I push the mattress up with my back and place it softly back on the bed and get the cover off the floor and try to remake it. Bonnie still never moves but her ears have come forward again and her tongue is hanging out the side of her mouth; she's panting a bit as I think she is now relaxing after holding her breath for the past three hours.

83

I stupidly decide to go and apologise to Dad, so I pull on some tracksuit bottoms, open the bedroom door and walk through to the living room.

Dad is sitting with his back to me, swaying in the chair, smoking his Regal King Size fag and guzzling his vodka and Coke. The table is all sticky where he's missed the glass while pouring vodka in it. He's watching a wildlife programme on gorillas and I'm half tempted to say, 'Do you miss your real family?' but I stop myself just in time. I have a habit of speaking my mind – a lot of people say it's cheek, but I prefer to be known as honest.

As I walk in, Dad snaps, 'What do yi want?' without looking away from the television.

'I'm sorry for what Bonnie's done, Dad.'

'What has Bonnie done, Charlie?'

'She did the toilet on the floor.'

Don't tell me he's forgotten already, I'm thinking.

'No, what has Bonnie done, Charlie?'

His voice is raised and I know this is one of his games. He wants me to say *shit* so he can waste me for swearing, not that he needs an excuse.

In for a penny in for a pound, I think, as I know very well what games he will play at different levels of being pissed.

'Bonnie shit on the floor, Dad.'

Oh! Oh! Here it comes.

'Correct Charlie, now go and clean it.'

It's weird but I think he wants me to swear, I think he finds it funny or something. Anyway I reverse out of the living room and go to the kitchen to get a cloth and some hot soapy water in a basin. I clean and scrub the carpet until it's gleaming. Meanwhile my face and neck are still covered in dog shit and Bonnie and my bed are in the same state.

I have to clean Bonnie first as she's bound to jump all around the house and I'll be cleaning for the next year. So I go into my bedroom.

'Come on, girl, bath time!'

Bonnie hates having a bath so I have to pick her up under her front legs with the back of her shit-covered head in my face.

I run a bath and get Bonnie cleaned and then wrap her in a towel and lock the bathroom door so she doesn't run around soaking everything while I'm in the bath. Next minute, *bang, bang, bang* on the door.

'What the fuck yi doing in there?'

'I'm in the bath, Dad.'

'Don't use all the fucking hot water, OK?' he says in a slurred voice.

Bonnie goes down on the floor with her ears back again and looks at me. 'It's OK, girl,' I say quietly, 'come here.'

She crawls across the floor like a sniper along the ground, not taking her eyes off me as he creaks back up the hall.

'Good job cleaning the carpet,' he slurs again.

The Nipper

Good job cleaning the carpet, you fucking weirdo. A few hours ago you wanted to kill me and my dog.

My anger's already getting bad at this stage of my life as I have taken that many beatings and all-night question sessions that I'm ready to explode.

Each time I go to Bonnie's aid after Dad has beaten her, Bonnie will strangely lift her left paw and lick my hands so that I can clean her eyes. The paw thing always confuses me – it's like she's making sure that I know he's beaten her. Maybe she's showing me that it's mentally affecting her too. I do what I think she wants me to do at the time though: I lick the paw that she's held up and it seems to make her feel better every time. She'll sit looking at me while I clean her eyes, her tail brushing the cold floor, knowing now that she is safe again. It isn't just a one-way thing – I help Bonnie to make the pain go and she does the same thing for me.

When I get home from school I'll get changed and then get Bonnie and take her out with me everywhere I go. Whether I'm playing football, hanging around the shops or even just sitting in a friend's back garden, people will ask me to show them what Bonnie would do if I was being attacked.

I have this party piece where I'll grab a tree or a metal lamppost and scream as if I were being attacked. Bonnie will stop whatever she's doing and come sprinting across the park and pounce on the tree, ripping the bark off, and if it's the lamppost you can hear her teeth clanging into the metal as she has it in a bearlike grip. It's a bit like watching a grizzly bear as when she's up on her back legs, the sheer height of her with her long black hair makes her look huge.

Bonnie also plays football with us – well, the game never lasts more than two minutes with her, which is normally the time it takes her to get hold of the ball. She tries to pick the ball up and run with it but her massive jaws and teeth will pierce through it like pins puncturing a balloon.

Bonnie and I also go to this place called Clatto Park at least four times a week. It's a big reservoir with two little islands in the middle with swans living on them most of the year. We both love it up there, Bonnie with her swimming and diving and me with the fresh air and watching people fishing. It's like a different world for us both.

Dad buys the cheapest, most horrible dog food on the planet. I honestly don't know how Bonnie keeps it down as it would easily knock a fly out sick, but Dad says it's the best value for its size. I think, in that case why don't you eat it then? Give Bonnie your dinner and you eat dirt cheap dog food on toast. As soon as you open a can you can smell it from outside in the garden. The smell's a cross between sweaty feet and herring. The actual food's meant to be rabbit, but it's more like one-year-old road kill.

Dad sometimes puts Bonnie on a metal chocker chain to take her to the shops when he goes for his vodka, Coke and cigarettes. I don't know why but somehow Bonnie always gets fed, even though her food's disgusting, as Dad's always sober when he feeds her around 2 p.m. I'm just unlucky that he'll wait until I get home before he flips his lid. Anything I do will set him off, even something as simple as not closing the garden gate on my way in – it's like he hates me and wants to pay me back for his childhood.

Bonnie is growing up fast and getting bigger and wiser. When I am getting a hiding she will quietly growl and show her teeth until he batters her and then I'll scream at him not to hit her, at which point he'll switch his attention back to me.

It's like a plan between us, me and Bonnie. We both try to get him exhausted so he's too knackered to keep going. It sometimes works, as he'll sit down and drink more vodka and get more pissed, and then fall over the table or settee trying to swing a punch. Then he'll just fall asleep where he lands and I'll take Bonnie out of the back garden for the loo then upstairs, back in the house and into my room where she cuddles up to me like a human.

The next day the usual will happen, the bedroom door will open and the usual rubbish will spill out of his lying, scarred face.

'I'll never drink again, son! I'm really sorry.'

Then he'll walk back out and I'll think, *One day you're going to die.*

Me and Bonnie look at each other with smirks on our faces as we know we're both getting bigger and he's getting weaker.

Some nights I will stand over him while he's sleeping, thinking of a way to kill him. Then the fear of him surviving will kick in, and I go back to bed, annoyed with myself for not doing it. He's in that much of a state some nights with drink, I am surprised he never kills himself by choking or pulling the electric fire onto himself, as he always falls asleep on the floor next to it.

Chapter Ten

Pressure Cooker

It's a warm, windy summer in Dundee. The year is 1985, I'm nine and Bonnie is just one year old by now and the bond between us is like no other. I know now why they call dogs 'man's best friend'.

It's about 4.30 p.m. and I've been home from school for about an hour and Dad's in the kitchen cooking stew in a massive pressure cooker. He makes a huge pot of stew so it will last all week; he'll spend his last £10 on all the ingredients and the rest goes on a supply of vodka and coke to last until Monday book day. He will also go and sweep a few chimneys if he's mega skint and needs voddy, as he calls it.

I pray every night that he'll fall off the roofs and break his neck, so I can watch him die. But he never does; he'll come home, black as the ace of spades, and wash his face, hair and hands in the kitchen sink before he has a bath. When I ask him why he does that, he tells me, 'If I don't it will leave a tidemark around the bath.'

The wallpaper is hanging off the wall, I'm thinking. The bathroom carpet is covered in piss where you've missed the bowl, and you're worried about a black ring going around the bath. Another one of your strange habits.

I've headed downstairs to see my pals outside in the close. Bonnie is upstairs in my room having a sleep and Dad is cooking dinner and reading the paper in the living room. One of the neighbours has asked him to come round to their house to take a look at something that needs fixing as he's quite handy at DIY. He's gone about five minutes and then goes back home to check on the stew.

When he gets to the kitchen Bonnie goes running past him and into my room, as she knows what she has done. I don't see Dad's reaction but I can hear him scream from outside, '*Noooo, you fucking bastard! no! no! no!*'

My heart sinks. *What have I done?* I run upstairs to find out what's going on. When I get to the door I hear, 'Yi're gonna fuckin' die, come here! *Get in there!*'

I open the door and the kitchen door slams up the hall on the left. He has dragged Bonnie into the kitchen and I can hear a metal clanging noise over and over again and a yelpy, squealing noise from Bonnie every time the metal clangs. I know he is hitting Bonnie so I run into the kitchen to see what's happening.

Whack! He turns the frying pan on me. I bounce back off the wall and look down in the corner at the dog. He has burst Bonnie's face open with the frying pan. Her eye has blood coming out of it, and her paws are bent under her body. Her jaw is twitching up and down and she's blinking rapidly.

'Please, Dad, stop! You're gonna kill her.'

'*What are we gonna eat the rest of the week?*' he screams at the top of his voice.

'I'll find something, Dad. Please don't kill her.'

But by this time he has noticed all the blood running down my face, as the frying pan blow has split the bit between my eyes open just above my nose. I can feel something warm running down my face but I think it's hot fat from the frying pan.

He then shoves me against the wall and turns and throws the frying pan at the dog. She lets out another yelp, even though it never hits her. She is shaking like a leaf and moaning, lifting one of her paws out from under her to show me what he has done. I've never seen a dog so scared.

He storms out of the house after that shouting, 'I'll have to go and borrow some money so yi two can eat, shan't I. *Bastards!*' Then the door slams. I dive on the ground with a cloth and try to stop the blood coming from her face, and her jaw keeps twitching. He must have hit one of her nerves, and it never ever goes away – from this time on there is always a twitch in Bonnie's jaw.

The next day I come home from school and I can hear *clang! clang! clang!* in the kitchen again. I panic and run in, but the dog is alone – she has the pressure cooker tied around her neck with a big thick wire.

At first I'm very confused: is this another one of his torture games? Apparently one of the neighbours has told him that if a dog chews a slipper or a shoe you should tie it around its neck, which would teach it not to do it again. I think the brutal hiding she got yesterday was warning enough, don't you?

I go into the living room where Dad is sitting and I don't say a word about the dog situation in the kitchen. I just say hello and go to get changed. A bit later we sit down in the living room and have something to eat. I think it's fish fingers, chips and beans.

I hate any kind of fish as my Granddad told me a story about when you go to the toilet and do your business, it all goes through sewage pipes to the ocean or sea and fish swim past shouting on their mate Bob in front, Bob! Bob! Bob! And all our shit ends up in their bellies. For years after hearing this I can't look at people eating fish as it makes me heave. I still don't eat it now!

Back in the living room it's quiet, everything is peaceful, Dad's not that drunk yet and it's fairly calm – and then all of a sudden, I hear the front door opening and a shout, 'Uncle Jock, Charlie, it's me.'

Oh shit, it's my cousin Shane. As you know, Shane always says exactly whatever happens to be on his mind. He just can't keep it in.

Clang! Clang! Clang! I can hear coming from the kitchen.

Bonnie knows Shane and wants to see him, but I'm praying to God that Shane just walks past the kitchen door and comes straight to the living room.

'Come in, Shane,' Dad shouts, but I hear the kitchen door opening and very faintly, 'Hiya, Bonnie', then a pause and then the kitchen door being closed, then the living-room door opens.

'Aright, Shane, what you up to?'

I'm trying to stare at him and tell him not to say anything about the dog. He sits down on the couch next to me.

'Hi, Uncle Jock.'

'Hi son, how's yir mum.'

That's Dad's sister, Aunt Molly. She's got dark hair and she's really pretty and bubbly.

'Yeah she's fine, the whole family are alright.'

Then it goes silent. We're watching *Countdown*. Richard Whiteley's wearing one of his deckchair jackets and a tie you'd need to wear massive Electra French sunglasses to cut down on the glare. Dad's trying to make words out of consonants and vowels. Meanwhile I'm sitting there praying that Shane has forgot about Bonnie, when these words I just do not want to hear come flowing out of Shane's mouth.

'Uncle Jock.'

'Yeah what is it?'

'Did you know your dog's got a pot tied around its neck?'

Well, I collapse, I simply fall apart. I don't know whether

to laugh or cry. I want the ground to swallow me up, and I can't control the contortions I go into. Then Shane starts giggling with little short sniggers.

'*Aghaa, teehee.*'

Well, that really finishes me off. The tears are running down my face, my cheekbones feel like they're poking through my skin, and my sides are more painful than after any beating I have ever had.

As always I'm looking to Dad to see what his reaction's going to be. Whatever happens, I look to Dad.

His face is impassive. I don't know which way he's going to go. Then suddenly he bursts out laughing.

'Yi're fucking mental,' he roars, 'there's definitely something not right aboot yi.'

'But Uncle Jock, there's a pot on her neck!'

I have to go out of the living room as I'm about to keel over. I have never laughed that much in my life, and at one point I even think I'm going to die from laughing as I can't breathe. I just never thought I would go that way.

I finally remove the pressure cooker from Bonnie's neck at two in the morning when Dad has fallen asleep. It must have driven her mad as it's huge.

Shane is a character and a half. His mum walked into the bathroom when he was young to see why he was taking so long washing his hair. When she looked at him she could see that he had emptied a whole bottle of shampoo on his head with no water. She asked him what the hell he was doing, and his reply was, 'It said on the bottle, "For dry hair only".'

He's the funniest kid on the planet, which he's proved on many occasions.

One morning I'm walking to school and I spot Shane walking up the path towards me with his head down. He is always tired as he does a paper round and a milk round before he comes to school. As he gets closer I look at his shoes, as one is brown and the other's black. When I point it out to him, he just keeps walking.

'I ken, I've got another pair like that in the hoose.'

I can't tell whether or not he really knows the absurdity of this, but I fall apart laughing.

Shane's one of those very rare nice kids. He never gets into fights, and when he gets older he never smokes, and hardly drinks, and always has a smile on his face.

One time we are throwing a football around in the living room in my house and Dad is in the bath. Shane knocks the plant pot off the windowsill. It lands upside down on the floor, soil everywhere.

Shane decides to shout through the bathroom door, 'Uncle Jock, the earth's fell oot the plant pot.'

'What did you fuckin' say?'

'The earth's fell oot the plant pot.'

'You wait until I get out this bath, I'm gonna smack your arse.'

The bathroom door opens and Dad is standing in a towel

ready to kick some ass.

'What did you just say, Shane?'

'The earth's fell oot of the plant pot.'

'Oh! The earth, I thought you said erse.'

That's a Dundee word for arse. It's a close shave for Shane.

'Your dad's fuckin' mental, eh,' he says.

'Yip,' I say.

Winter has arrived again and I'm searching through some local back gardens near St Fillans Road for a shovel. I have devised a plan to get some fast cash to feed my empty belly through the winter months. I've seen some of the older lads getting paid for cleaning the snow away from people's front doors and paths and I want a piece of it.

Some mornings the snow will be so deep that it covers the bottom half of the door and old people who live alone end up stuck inside. I start on the first house and you can only see the top of my head, then clumps of snow flying up in the air at an alarming pace. My nose, ears and fingertips are numb but I don't care as the thought of a chip butty from the St Giles chip shop is making me fly like the wind.

When I finish, the old man pays me one pound and I sprint down towards the shops, dragging my new work tool behind me. I take my chip butty outside and sit on the cold metal fence where I lean my shovel. The butter from the chip roll has now melted and is pouring down my chin as I try to cram the whole thing in my mouth in case anyone asks for a bite.

Then as the heat of the chips starts to warm my insides, I get ready to resume phase two of my split shift.

I go back and forward for the next couple of hours until my belly can't take any more. I'm now standing outside the chippy again with a huge smile on my face, only this time I'm leaning on the fence trying to keep down what I have just devoured. This is a serious case of eyes being bigger than belly. It's times like this when I wish I were a hamster. Most people I know hate the feeling of being stuffed with food but not me; the feelings of hunger I have some nights make this seem heavenly.

Cleaning snow from doors is only one of my money making survival schemes. I have another easy tax-free way to fill my boots. I think I'm a bit like a meerkat with this one; I go foraging at the back of shops and the supermarket for empty glass bottles. I take a bin liner and collect all the bottles to take down the local shop and cash them in for ten pence each. This is easy money as I find around twenty, then it's back to the chippy for a Wallace pie – my Holy Grail. Nothing on the planet can ever get near the taste of a Wallace pie, it feels like a little part of heaven is here on earth.

The grease is dripping down my chin onto my hand and when I finish I spend a few minutes licking the salt and vinegar from the paper until it is all gone. Now I can head home and take a beating with a full belly. At least now it won't feel as bad.

The final money-spinner for me as a nine year old is

Operation Spondoolies. If I'm unsuccessful with foraging for bottles or if last night's rain has washed away the snow, I have an alternative method of collecting cash. Dundee is full of red, Tardis-like telephone boxes as hardly anyone can afford a house phone, so armed only with a cardboard box I set off on a mission to stuff and block every hole that the money is returned from with bits of card.

Late in the evening I go back round and collect the loot that was stuck inside by reaching my skinny fingers up inside. Some nights I can make up to ten quid. I exchange all the coins for a ten pound note at the shop and hide it in my sock before I go home – I don't want Dad, to find it, do I?

I wonder if my real family are actually called Trotter, not Mitchell. We do have similar homes and décor, after all.

Chapter Eleven

Inside an Igloo with a Drunk Bear

One night during the school summer holidays while I'm still living at St Fillans Road, Dad and his brother, Uncle Danny, are having a bevy in the house after the pubs have closed and the babysitter has gone home and I'm tucked up in bed.

Danny's a really nice guy and I always get on well on with him – he's a very funny man. But Dad and Danny hate each other and fight all the time. I think they fight over what Dad is doing to me. One night I hear Danny shout, 'You fucking animal,' and it's definitely about me.

But I love it when Dad has parties and has people around because I won't get touched. Instead he always ends up fighting with people in the house. I'm fine though because me and Bonnie are safe. We just sleep through it.

They've been drinking all night and finally I hear the front door close about eight in the morning and then silence. I get up to investigate but there's no one there, not even Dad. I switch on the TV and go in the kitchen to get some toast and milk for breakfast, and open a can of corned beef for Bonnie and put it in her bowl. Then I go into the living room to watch cartoons until 8.30. The house is peaceful and everything is calm, then like a whirlwind Dad and Danny come crashing up the hall and into the living room where I'm sitting. They're both covered in blood.

'If the polis come, we've been sleepin'. Yi tell them we've been here all night.'

'OK, Dad.' I run and get a quilt from the bedroom to throw over them.

Two minutes later, four policemen come crashing through the front door. I'm now standing at the living-room door with my hands on each part of the frame.

'What are you doing, mister?' I ask the police.

'Where's yir dad and his mate?'

'They're in there sleeping. They've been here all night having a party.'

They push me out of the way and walk into the lounge as I hang on the tallest one's leg trying to protect my patch. They walk over to the couch and pull the quilt back. Dad and Uncle Danny are both covered in blood, pretending they're asleep. 'Jock, you can stop pretending. We seen you run away from the car and come up here, and you're gonna need a few stitches for that head.'

Uncle Danny is still pretending he's out cold and Dad's saying, 'What, eh, what's going on? I've just woke up.'

I can see the coppers laughing at the fact that they're still trying to say it wasn't them. They had taken the car to go and get some fags from the garage but they were that drunk that on the way back they drove it into a lamppost at the bottom of St Fillans Road and nearly smashed someone's house wall down. They didn't even have seat belts on. I just wish that Dad had been going faster and Uncle Danny had had his belt on.

They are taken away by the police and social services come up to look after me, but one of the neighbours says they'll look after me until Dad gets back out later in the day.

This happens a few times: police will come to the door for Dad and Uncle Danny or looking for some of his other mates. I'm dying to tell them that he's torturing me every time they come, but I know he won't be done for it, as he always seems to slither his way out of it, using me as an excuse. And when someone tells you they'll kill you, you kind of learn to keep your trap shut.

Sometimes Dad goes for a party at different mates' houses and I have to go with him if he has no babysitter. He always takes the car with him, even though he's banned and is obviously going to get drunk.

It's a couple of days before New Year's Eve and his mate Hatchy is having a shindig at his house in Ardler. There's a big long row of flats behind the shops – I think everyone I know lives in flats behind shops. Hatchy lives bottom left in the middle one. His house is quite smart for an Eighties' pad – it's clean, shall we say.

The good thing about being a nipper with an alcoholic dad is that when you're dragged to some house party, you can wander about doing what you like, as the grown-ups are that hammered that they don't give a shit.

The party's going fine for the first few hours, then the usual riots start.

'Yi owe me a tennar frae last week,' says Dad.

'I gave that back on Tuesday or Wednesday,' replies Hatchy.

'No yi fuckin never.'

'Ah shut yir puss you two,' someone pipes in.

'Wha er you talkin' ti, yi prick?'

'Oh are yi goin' ti start trouble we a drink on yi again?'

'Keep yir fuckin nose oot o'it, it's fuck all ti dae we yo.'

It calms down for a minute and then Dad starts up again.

'Dinna try and embarrass me again in front o' company or I'll belt yir puss.'

'For fuck's sake, Jock. Forget aboot it.'

'Ney wonder, fuckin' half-wit.'

'Wha's a fuckin' half-wit?'

The next moment four fully grown paralytic Scotsmen are in what looks like a scrum, falling over the settee and television, knocking over the plants and sending a table full of drinks flying as they all go through it.

Meanwhile I'm standing there, a nine-year-old kid, leaning against the door with someone's can of Export, dying to join in. And with Hatchy's wife screaming, '*Stop it yi fucking idiots, there's kids here.*'

It's more of a wrestling match than a fight – every man for himself. They are that drunk that by the time it has all calmed down they never have a clue about what they've just been kicking lumps out of each other for.

'*Get oot this fucking hoose the lot o yi!*' screams Hatchy's wife who is going mental, but nobody's listening. They just put the music back on – it's ZZ Top – open another can and start trying to dance around all the broken glass, 'cause every girl's crazy 'bout a sharp dressed man.

It's now three in the morning and Dad decides that he has to get home. He gets up off the couch, checking his pockets for the car keys and swaying from side to side then back and forward, eyes half-closed and a line of blood on his white shirt pocket from earlier, someone else's I think.

'Come on, Charlie, get your coat.'

Everyone else is sleeping except Hatchy.

'I'll get you a taxi, Jock,' he says.

'No, no, no, no. I'm alright, I'm alright, I've got transport.'

Dad's slurring his words even more now as it's getting later and he's getting more tired.

'I'm off, come on Charlie.'

'See ya Hatchy,' I say with a yawn.

'See ya, wee man.'

I walk behind Dad as he sways from side to side, walking in the opposite direction from where his car is.

'Dad, it's this way.'

'I ken war my fucking car is.'

He obviously doesn't as it's right outside the door on the left and he's turned right, but I'm not gonna argue.

'Some bastard's moved my car. I parked it over here.'

'It's back there, Dad look.'

'I canna believe some bastard's moved my car, *bastards*.'

He turns around and I just shuffle behind him and follow on again. It's absolutely freezing. Dundee in the winter is bad enough but at three in the morning it's like the North Pole. I remember one of Dad's mates saying when he was young, he woke up with an ice cube in his bed and when he threw it in the coal fire it made a fart noise. I've always thought that was hilarious.

We get in the car and all the windows are covered with ice. It's like being in an igloo with a drunk bear. It takes Dad ages to get his key in the ignition and I'm getting colder by the minute but I can't say anything because any remark from me could set him off. After about five minutes of silence and me blowing mist out of my mouth to keep myself entertained, Dad turns around to me with his left eye closed, trying to focus.

'What, do you want to fucking drive?'

I never say anything as I've managed to learn when to speak and when not to speak, depending on how drunk he is.

He turns away again and hallelujah – the key goes in and the car starts. The windows are covered in ice and I still can't see a thing. He turns the wipers on and shouts, 'We have lift-off.'

I try not to laugh just in case he actually thinks he is in a plane, as we might as well be in a submarine for all he knows.

'Turn the heaters on, I canna see a fucking thing.'

I'm not surprised with all the scotch and vodka you've been drinking.

Then he starts singing, 'Can yi hear the Rangers sing, I canna see a fucking thing woowoooo!'

He's actually lost the plot, I think. I switch the heaters on and the window wipers are going full speed.

'Your lights, Dad.'

'I'm no fucking daft,' he says, turning the wipers back off. That's his attempt at putting the lights on.

No you're not daft, that will help you see in the dark, you stupid plonker.

Luckily I don't say this out loud. Eventually the window starts to clear and he finds the lights. He's looking more and more wobbly as time goes on, probably down to the fact that we've been in the car for fifteen minutes and not even moved an inch. I'm freezing and getting a bit tired myself as I hardly slept the night before.

Then we start moving. We drive out of the car park at about five miles an hour onto the main road at the back of Ardler and turn right towards Downfield Golf Course, passing the turning for the Timex Brae. Dad is now muttering away to himself, 'And away we go.' The car's all over the road and Dad's head is kind of bobbing up and then slowly falling down.

Shit, I think, *he's falling asleep.*

'Dad, Dad! You're falling asleep!'

He doesn't respond.

'*Dad!* You're falling asleep,' I shout a second time.

Nothing again, so I grab the wheel as we're coming up to a massive bend to the right up the side of the golf course. I hold on for dear life while he takes forty winks with his foot planted on the accelerator.

I don't know how I manage it, but I steer the car up past the Ardler multi-storey block and up towards Clatto Park. It's a thousand metres and all the time I'm screaming at the top of my lungs, '*Dad, wake up you're in your car, Dad! Dad! Wake up!*'

I even muster the courage to elbow him in the side of the head – and that seems to do the trick.

'Oh hello!' he shouts as he wakes up, and looks at me all confused. 'What the fuck's going on!'

'Look at the road, Dad, you fell asleep, you're driving.'

He looks at my hand on the wheel then looks forward and puts his hands on the wheel.

'Fuck me, I'm pissed,' he says, turning right down into St Kilda Road and back towards St Fillans to the house, clipping wing mirrors all the way home.

Brilliant, I think, the fiasco's over. My heart's still pounding, and now he's trying to squeeze the car into an eight foot gap. It takes him twenty minutes and he keeps nudging one car and then the other until he creates enough space for himself. He keeps saying, 'Tell me when I'm close to the other car.'

He pushes the cars out of the way and there's now exhaust smoke everywhere, and the noise of him revving is deafening.

We've spent fifty minutes doing a four-minute car journey and the cold air has sobered him up from being paralytic to that horrible cock-eyed stare he gives me when he's pissed off. To make matters worse, Bonnie has pissed on the carpet, as she hasn't been out all day or night and it's now nearly four in the morning.

Dad walks into the kitchen and I go into the bedroom to check on Bonnie. She has her head squeezed under a six-inch gap under my bed with her body sticking out. I can hear Dad getting his vodka out of the cupboard and closing the fridge door where he keeps his Coke.

'Charlie, get in here.' His voice has changed to that horrible, familiar tone I dread. 'Bring that fucking fleabag in here as well.'

'Stay there girl,' I say to Bonnie and close the bedroom door behind me and walk up the hall into the living room.

'Sit over there.'

I walk over and sit on the couch.

'Turn the TV on.'

I grab the remote and take it off standby and then sit back down.

He doesn't say anything for five long minutes. He just keeps swaying and sipping his voddy.

'What's this shite you've put on?' he hisses.

'I don't know, Dad, I'll change it.' I reach for the remote.

'Leave it.'

Here we go, I think. But Bonnie's safe – he's forgotten about her.

'Do yi ken something, yi're no even my son, you live here but your Uncle Danny is your real dad. Yir mum thinks she's got one over on me.'

He's slurring his words and pouring more vodka from his half-empty litre bottle.

'What are yi fucking looking at me for? It's not my fault.'

I'm thinking, *I hope that's true, you evil bastard.*

'What are yi doing here anyway? You don't live here. Nobody ever wanted yi, that's how I got palmed off with yi. Jock the mug, he'll look after somebody's runt.'

Tears are running down my face. I feel like nothing, less than nothing, worse than I've ever felt. Like I've been shoved into the bottom of a deep well, and mud and dirt and filth and excrement have been shovelled on top of me. I can't get any lower.

There's a seething, burning rage in me, a mixture of anger and hurt, and I'll never forget this moment. But I can't challenge him to a scrap, even though I want to smash that vodka bottle and cut his throat with it. Dad sits forward in his chair and I know what's about to happen. He starts by picking things up off the table and throwing them at me, the usual stuff like remote controls, lighters, ashtrays, ketchup bottles or salt containers that have been left from tea three days before.

Then he stands up and staggers towards me with a fag in one hand and his right hand clenched. I lie back on the couch and cover myself up, cringing from him, as the fag he's smoking is getting closer and closer. He punches me in the thighs and ribs with his right hand, and all I can do is cover my face, and take the blows on the rest of my body. Then I feel this sting on my thumb, this horrible pain. He has tried to shove his fag into my eyes through my hands but he only catches my thumb, and all the sparks and the head of the fag go down my top and burn my chest.

I'm screaming in agony but that seems to make him worse. He definitely gets off on people cowering and screaming. I know for a fact he enjoys it. He keeps on going, smashing plants on my head, kicking me, punching me and dragging me around the room by the hair, kneeing me in the side of the head. There's blood everywhere. I'm trying to drag myself behind the couch while he's stamping on the back of my legs.

Then it stops. He's having a breather and getting another drink of vodka.

I lie there in agony, trying to squeeze my smashed-up head between the couch and wall, a bit like Bonnie earlier. I feel his hand on my hair again, yanking me upwards. He is so pissed he falls backwards over the coffee table with me; I land on top of him looking up at the ceiling as if I'm lying on an operating table. I scramble up and stagger towards the door, pull it closed behind me, and then run into my room.

I close the bedroom door and try to drag the bed beside it to jam it shut, but my arms are aching and I can hardly stand from the stamps on my calves. I just managed to drag an old brown chest of drawers across the room and wedge it between the end of the bed and the wall. He'll have to get a chainsaw to cut the door in half to get in here now.

I lie on the floor beside Bonnie in the corner of the room and she starts licking all the blood off my face and her ears stand up pointed at every sound Dad makes as he walks to the toilet past my door.

He's back in the living room, bouncing off the walls, mumbling and singing to himself, playing 'You Really Got Me' by the Kinks on the record player – you got me so I can't sleep at night. It's really loud and he's trying to sing along to Ray Davies, and it's horrible. Sometimes it's Sinatra, sometimes Lionel Richie, but it's always horrible. How nobody ever comes to my rescue even one night I will never know. Somebody must have heard at least one of the times.

Maybe people just get used to the sound of a dog barking at the moon in the middle of the night.

The next day around 9 a.m. I hear a movement in the living room. I can also hear a record needle skipping – you know when the arm and needle go to the middle when you don't change the record. I can hear the floorboards creak as he comes up the hall.

Then I see the handle on the door go down but he doesn't shout at me as he normally would. The handle just slowly goes back up. He must think I'm sleeping, but I didn't sleep a wink last night, I just watched the door for hours and every time he got up to go for a pee I could feel my heart pounding through my blood-soaked top.

At the age of nine I've already more or less lost the will to live. Dad's out of control and has stopped saying sorry the next day. I'll wake up in the morning and he'll still have a drink in his hand, with the music playing full blast. I think he's turned into an alcoholic to block out all the bad things he's done, as he can't face reality. Drinking is never going to solve anything, but his plan is to drown his worries in a sea of vodka.

Occasionally there are moments of respite with Dad, times when I can even laugh with him, even though they are few and far between. Dad is a full-blown alcoholic by now, but he always manages to get up the roofs the next day, as he's still sweeping chimneys. Sometimes he takes me with him, and makes me hold the covers against the fireplace inside while he goes on the roof and sweeps it from the top. I chat away to all the old people about back in the day. Old ladies tell me stories of when they were young.

'We had to climb up the chimney years ago.'

'How did yi manage ti fit up there, misses?'

'Not this chimney, we had bigger ones back then.'

I just stand there, biting my lip, trying to stop myself asking her – how it would be possible for a fourteen-stone woman to fit up an eight-inch gap.

Then Dad's voice comes down the chimney: 'OK!'

That means he has finished, and I can take the covers out to clean the soot. But one time, when I take them out and look in the fireplace, there's nothing there! Not a bit of soot in sight.

Dad has come down from the roof and walks into the room where I'm standing.

'It's empty, Dad.'

'What di yi mean, it's empty?'

'There's nae soot in it, Dad.'

Suddenly there's a knock at the front door and the woman who owns the house goes to get it. Dad's looking at me with a smirk on his face, as he has now realised what he's done. I can hear a shout from down the hall, as the woman opens the door.

'*Jesus Christ Mary*, what happened to you?'

I walk over to the living-room door to have a look at what's going on. Then I see it. This four-foot woman's standing there, with a black Scottish terrier dog in her arms, that obviously used to be white. The woman has two white circles on her eyes where her glasses must have been and she's covered from head to toe in black soot.

I walk back behind the door into the living room and nearly collapse. The tears are running down my face, and my body is shaking uncontrollably as I try to hold my laughter in. She looks like a panda, and the dog is sneezing like mad.

'What's happened, Mary?'

'I was sitting at the fire knitting a jumper, and the next minute a massive cloud of smoke hit me in the face. It's ruined my room.'

Well, that's it. Even Dad has a smile on his face and I'm now in a heap on the floor, trying not to think of her big panda eyes while Dad walks up the hallway to explain why he has swept the wrong chimney.

It takes us four hours to clean that old lady's house but it's worth every minute.

I wake up the next morning still laughing, as it's the funniest thing I have ever seen.

Dad has started taking me to a few jobs with him now and is also giving me new missions to go on. They range from spying in his girlfriend's house window at three in the morning

114

with a ladder to see if she has a man there, to climbing on roofs to steal gas caps and Chinese hats from the chimney pots.

He's now getting some use out of me and I'd rather be out at three in the morning stealing than at home with him drunk. It's great now, I'm actually getting some brownie points for breaking the law. I am feeling as if I have a purpose in life, scaling the rooftops like a cat and climbing up tall chimney stacks like a chimp, hugging it like a member of Greenpeace with an old oak tree.

Dad also takes me out in the car while he's drunk, picking up sets of ladders or timber that he's spotted while out on his travels earlier in the day. Dad seems like an alien being to me – he seems to have his own rules from his own planet. It's a planet where people breathe Dundee smog instead of oxygen, their blood is made from vodka and they beat their kids up for sport.

And there's no way off this planet.

Chapter Twelve

The Swag Factory

I'm now ten years old and in the years that I've been apart from Mum and my brothers, there have been a couple of times when Dad has tried to get rid of me by giving me away.

Once he tries to give me to his mum – my Gran – because he can't cope, or so he says, although he's beating me up at the time as usual, so as far as I'm concerned he's coping in the way he's always coped – by using me as a punch bag. I feel relieved to get away, excited, and at the same time anxious at the thought of leaving Dad and going to live with my grandparents. It would be such a huge change in my life.

Of course I should feel unwanted and unloved and rejected, but by this time nothing surprises me about Dad's behaviour towards me and I mainly think it's just another of his games to torment me. But at the same time I'm also wondering how am I going to cope with being stuck with two old people who I hardly really know, and am sad about not being able to see my friends at school, which up to now has been my only escape from the hell I've been going through.

But as it turns out, Gran doesn't take me because she's an old woman by now and it would just be too much for her. When Dad tells me that I'm not going to live with Gran and Granddad I experience an odd feeling of disappointment mixed with relief. I think it's a case of better the devil you know than the one you don't. Dad's world is scary enough – who knows what lies beyond it? – or maybe that's what I think at the time. Then when I'm eight he suddenly tells me he's going to give me to my mum.

I don't know what to think or how to feel about this. It's so long since I last saw my mum – I was only four years old – and I've almost forgotten what she looks like. Besides, even though I live in constant fear of what Dad will do to me next, I'm used to being with him.

I'm also frightened of going to see my mum again as in the back of my mind I still believe what Dad told me when I was four – that if my mum gets her hands on me again she'll try to kill me. Since that time I've almost forgotten her – out of sight is out of mind for me – and the only feeling I've had about her is that I should stay away from her. If my dad's a monster, I've told myself, she must be even worse.

But I don't dare disobey Dad and he keeps saying, 'Yi'll be alright, son, don't you worry.'

The Nipper

So there I am, eight years old, and I go and spend a weekend with my mum. Dad drops me off on Friday evening without waiting to speak to Mum and when she opens the front door, I can see she's overwhelmed to see me again and is finding it difficult not to cry. She reaches down to hug me and I instinctively flinch away. I don't mean to, I can't help it, but I have no way of dealing with this show of affection from someone who's more or less a stranger to me. Besides, I'm not used to experiencing any kind of physical contact from an adult that isn't a beating. It's all too much for me.

I can see that she's a little hurt by this, although she tries to hide it as she takes me into the house. I recognise her face but it's like I've dreamt about her. She still has those blue eyes and blonde hair. But I can see that her eyes are sad – maybe I was too young to remember those sad eyes when I was not yet four years old, or maybe her sadness has grown over the years.

On the whole though she's bright, funny and full of life and wants to make up for all those years with lots of questions. She keeps asking me about Dad and whether he's looking after me and what he gives me to eat and in no time at all I'm finding it very hard to cope with all these questions. It's all too different and strange, and I don't know which way to act.

Besides, I think I'm still a little confused. Who is this person and what does she really want of me? Is she suddenly going to turn, like Dad does, and beat me? And are all these questions just the start of an interrogation session that will make Dad's Gestapo nights seem like a tea party? Also I don't quite know how to answer her questions as I'm scared that if I don't answer them correctly the consequences will be even more dire than with Dad.

There are also other things about being in this strange house that have thrown me. For one thing, apart from Tommy, who I hardly remember, there's my six-year-old younger brother Bobby who I don't know at all, and there's a new man – not Blake, her second husband, who I never really knew in any case, but a man called Dale. I'm not used to him and I'm not ready for any of this. I'm too used to living in captivity with Dad, too used to my prison.

The contrast between life in Mum's house and life in Dad's couldn't be greater. Mum's house is spotless and smells like flowers. There's never a dish in the sink or a cup on the side as she's a very clean and tidy woman. I suppose I notice this particularly as it's so different to the filth and squalor I'm used to with Dad. And there are all these people, Mum, Dale, Tommy, Bobby. They all talk to each other in ways I'm not used to at home. What is it that seems so different? It's all so low key, for a start, quiet and friendly, a lot of bantering but it's easy bantering, too easy for me. There must be something wrong. Something I don't understand and no one's explaining to me. They must be up to something.

Another thing I can't cope with is eating with my mum and her family. We all sit down together to eat at a table and that also unnerves me. It hardly ever happens at home with Dad. The plates and knives and forks are all sparkling clean, and she's made this special meal for me with all these vegetables I've never eaten at home with Dad, though we do get greens at school. And there's tomatoes. I hate tomatoes but I daren't tell her that; I just concentrate on the rest of the food, the lamb chops and new potatoes and roast potatoes and peas and rice and cauli and carrots and gravy which are all actually delicious and suddenly I'm wolfing it all down.

She keeps stopping me and saying, 'It's like you've never eaten before.'

What she doesn't realise is what my eating regime is like with Dad. When I'm at home I don't even eat some nights. I'm as thin as a sprat so I can't defend myself against him. I'm never allowed to eat until he says and if he falls asleep I don't dare move. So I just conk out and wake up in the morning and then I'll be off school if he's battered me and he'll give me one piece of toast and then I'll just be starving all day until I get my free dinner ticket next lunch time – I even love the lukewarm, lumpy semolina you get for pudding. Then he'll be drunk again and I won't eat until lunch the next day or two days if I'm off school and Dad has totally lost it on me.

By that time I've started to see things that aren't there. I later find out the word is 'hallucinating' and when you're getting beaten up and go without any food your brain starts to hallucinate. You just don't know what's going on. I some-times put cushions over my stomach to stop the rumbling – that's how loud my stomach can be.

When she puts me to bed – I'm sleeping in Tommy's bed as he's agreed to sleep in a camp bed next to it for the night – Mum asks me if I would like her to read me a bedtime story. I don't know what to say as I've never had one of those before, so I just shake my head and mutter no thanks and she reads a story to Bobby instead.

The next day, Saturday, I'm still feeling anxious and over-whelmed as I'm not used to living in a house with all these people. But I manage to get through it and in the afternoon Tommy and I play football in the local park, which is the best thing so far about the weekend. But the following day, Sunday, I suddenly panic. I'm thinking about what Dad might do to me if I'm not at home for all this time and I finally flip and run away from her house in Charleston, which is about four miles from Dundee, all the way back to St Fillans Road. For the first bit of the run my brother Tommy chases me but I manage to give him the slip. Then he finds me hid-ing behind a shed in a back garden. He asks me why I've run away and begs me to come back, but I can't as I simply want to be back in captivity where things are familiar.

When I get back home to the filth and squalor and chaos that is Dad's flat at St Fillans Road, it's back to the Gestapo grilling with Dad asking me, hour after hour, about my mum and what I've said about him.

Dad keeps on, questioning and beating me, until I tell him what he wants to hear. Which is whatever twisted version of the truth he feels like getting me to say.

'So did yir mum hit yi like I always told yi she would?'

'No, Dad.'

'So yi're calling me a liar, eh?'

'No Dad, I mean, you're not a liar, but she didn't hit me.'

'Which is it?'

'I don't know, Dad.'

'What d'yi mean, yi don't know? Yi don't know if she hit you like this—'

He hits me in the stomach and sends me flying across the floor.

'Is she or is she not an evil fucking bitch?'

'Yes Dad.'

'Yes what?'

'Yes Dad, she's an evil fucking bitch.'

'Are you swearing aboot yir own mother?'

'No.'

'Am I deaf then? Did my ears deceive me?'

After several hours of this I have no idea what I'm saying any more and he's managed to beat a false confession out of me, which by now I'm even believing myself because by this time I don't know what is the truth and what isn't. I just have to remember not to swear as that will just be one more opportunity for him to keep on taunting me.

'She's a bitch, she's a bitch, Dad, a horrible, nasty evil bitch, and I never want to see her again.'

Dad smirks. He's got what he wanted. He's like a policeman who's managed to pin a crime on an innocent suspect. He's got a result.

For months afterwards I put the whole experience of going to see Mum, what Dad forced me to say about her, and my mixed up confusion about the whole thing to the back of my mind, but now, two years later, I'm getting curious about my mum and brothers and I keep wishing I hadn't run away that last time. Besides, my mum and dad have been speaking on the phone and have decided that it's unfair to keep me and my brother apart because, apart from that weekend when I was eight, we haven't seen each other for around six years. But Mum still remembers what Dad was like when they were together all those years ago and is very cautious about sending Tommy over to spend the night.

By this time I'm dying to tell someone what's been going on with Dad – what he's been doing to me. When I was eight it didn't occur to me to do that – I was far too frightened to tell. But now I want someone to notice. It's been brewing up in me for the last two years.

A few weeks after my last visit to my mum the penny finally dropped: I put two and two together and realised that Dad had blatantly lied to me when he'd told me that my mum had tried to kill me and that if she saw me again she'd try to do the same thing. This had been sitting in the back of my mind ever since I was a nipper, not even five years old, when Dad had snatched me and I'd then chosen him to live with. It was probably the reason why I did choose him, because before I could even put words to it, he'd been telling me my mum was evil.

But after the visit when I was eight it was clear as daylight that Mum couldn't hurt a fly, that she wasn't that evil person, and that she had always loved me and cared about me and had wanted me all those years.

And this time, once I go and stay with her, I know almost instantly that Dad has been lying to me, and I'm filled with remorse and anger that I had allowed the wool to be pulled over my eyes all these years. I discover that all through those years she has always wanted me back. I didn't know it at the time, but she was fighting for me every way she could. She tells me she's written letters, tried to ring him – even my Aunt Molly, Dad's sister – has tried to intercede on her behalf – but Dad has always stonewalled her, and of course Dad never mentioned any of this to me. When I realise this it breaks me up inside.

Why did I believe his lies? But he's always been very clever at making me believe what he wants me to believe. I feel torn apart and upset at the deception and at what might have been. I feel like I've already wasted my life.

Mum soon puts me straight about what happened between them back then when she and Dad broke up. She tells me

Dad kicked her out in the snow when she was pregnant with Tommy and that none of her own family would take her in: as far as they were concerned she had made her bed leaving home and getting pregnant, so she could now lie in it.

She was freezing and scared about being out all night so she turned to my Aunt Molly who was also pregnant. She took Mum in for a few days until Dad would let her come back. Women in those days had no chance in society.

She must have been very down and depressed when she broke up with Dad but she somehow got through it and I think that's what's made her such a strong character now. She could have gone under and resorted to drink, but her attitude was, 'He left me in a worse state that anybody could have left anybody but he would have won if I'd just given in to it and ended up a drinker like him.' She coped and she was determined not to be beaten by him.

By now Mum has remarried for the third time – the first was Dad and the second was Blake, who was the dad of my younger brother Bobby. He's a good kid, Bobby, but still too young to know what's going on in life. He's eight now – the age I was when I ran away from Mum's.

Her third husband is Dale. I get on well with him – he's a bricklayer, tall, placid and easy-going, someone who likes a quiet life.

When I see what Mum's really like, I feel guilty for having thought badly of her. But to be honest, before seeing her again all I've thought about for most of those six years between the ages of four and ten was myself – it's been all about whether I'm going to die or if Dad will die. I haven't thought about my mum or my gran or my brothers – even though I've missed my brother Tommy.

We have half a brain each – that's what everyone says once we get together again – and I'm remembering that from when we were young. I'm now starting to remember how I felt like a twin who had been torn away from his other half and that's the only thing that really got to me at first about going with Dad instead of Mum when I was four.

Tommy and I start staying together for nights – at Mum's one weekend and at Dad's the next. And having been separated for six years, when we finally meet each other again we bond like the long-lost brothers we are. We even finish each other's sentences, just like twins, only he's two years older than me. If he has an idea to go and do something I am already packed and raring to go.

The things Tommy and I get up to are unbelievable. We're a bit like a juvenile version of the Krays. We take a couple of golf clubs and a torch into the woods sometimes looking for rabbits with Mixy – it's a disease that leaves rabbits blind. We'll shine the torch in the rabbit's eyes and then smack! The golf club head will connect with the rabbit's head and, hey presto, it's out of its misery.

Even though this anger is building up inside me I still kill those rabbits out of kindness, whereas Tommy really seems to enjoy whacking their heads off. You can see it in his eyes, that he has something eating him inside as well. As I later find out, Mum has told him what Dad did to all of us when he was young and although I'm the one who has been bullied and battered all these years, Tommy is outraged and bitter about Dad and it's getting to him as much as it gets to me.

Tommy has a different personality from me. He isn't able to cope with things like I've learnt to. His attitude once he knows what Dad has done is: how dare he, the fucking bastard, I won't let him get away with it. He's a great brother to have but once he's angry there's no saying what he'll do.

When Tommy stays over with me at Dad's it's better for me as far as beatings from Dad are concerned, at least to begin with. I can see that Dad's on his guard in the early days, putting up a kind of wary but peaceable front for Tommy's sake. But you can see that look behind Dad's eyes. The sudden turn, the nasty, evil side when he gets drunk, he can't hide it and Tommy soon starts to see what he's really like. For a long time though he doesn't beat me when Tommy's around.

Tommy in turn is obviously scared of Dad, but not nearly as scared of him as I am, and as the months go by, the bottled-up hostility and hatred on both sides comes bubbling to the surface. Tommy's much more fiery than I am and will stand his ground with Dad and occasionally answer him back, but he's still too young to beat him in a fight so he manages to keep an uneasy peace with Dad. But they're both watching each other, watching and waiting. Sometimes you could cut the mood between them with a knife.

A lot of young kids we know, including us, are being treated so badly and abused so much that it has turned a whole generation into time bombs, just waiting to go off. They would (including me) attack and destroy anything in their path.

We're only kids but most adults would regard some of the games we play as horrendous and would certainly have complained to the RSPCA – though we simply find them fun. They include putting live frogs on barbecues, and inserting a straw up a frog's backside and blowing it up like a balloon until it explodes. One of Tommy's friends has drawn a circular target on a wooden garden shed with blackboard chalk. We've found a birds' nest in a hedge with chicks in it and decide to throw the chicks at the target.

When Tommy and I start spending more time together we stay at Mum's every other weekend. Her house is in a place in Charleston called Butters Loan. She's been there for a few years. Mum still has blonde hair and her blue eyes are as bright as ever. Not surprisingly, she's much smaller than I remember her and she always wears a lot of jewellery, including a gold cross and real gold bracelets. You can hear them jangle when she does the dishes.

Mum doesn't go to church and we're not practising Catholics – though I do get confirmed as a Catholic and occasionally go to church when I'm at school, for instance at Christmas. When she gets drunk she's nuts – out of control – but in a silly, joky way not a violent way like Dad. She's very upfront and outspoken and speaks her mind, so if someone's telling her their story and she knows they're lying, she won't be diplomatic – she'll just say 'What are yi lying for?'

She's fearless like I am when I'm not around Dad. She just doesn't care. You can say, I think you're out of order and she'll just say fine. But in any case I adore my mum, and worship her to bits. Now I know the truth I don't blame her for not getting me back all those years. I know she fought for me every way she could and at this time I don't blame her either as I've never even thought about not having a mum – it's never even bothered me.

When she goes out for the night with friends we have a babysitter who's about eighteen and who's supposed to look after us for the night. Dale goes out with his friends and Mum goes out with hers, but half the time the babysitter seems to be zonked out on dope and pills or whatever else she takes with her boyfriend and always seems to crash out around ten o'clock watching TV. That's when Tommy and I make our exit. We lower ourselves out of the second-floor back window of our bedroom, narrowly missing the washing line in the back green. It's pitch black at this time of night as it's an enclosed grassy area behind four sets of tenement blocks, which form a sort of square.

We synchronise our watches to get back into the house before 2.15 a.m. as Mum gets in between 2.30 and 3 a.m. We're so organised for these escapades that we even carry torches on us during the day. I think Tommy always has to be prepared for sticky situations as the places we explore are often pretty dark and dingy.

On this particular night when we climb out of the window I don't have even a clue where we're going. Tommy's the man with the plan and I'm his tagalong sidekick. It feels fantastic having a big brother again – I hadn't realised how much I've missed him all these years – especially as he's so crazy and fearless.

'Come on, Charlie, get off your arse.'

When I drop out of the window I fall backwards and land in a load of mud that Mum's next-door neighbour has dug up for worms when he goes fishing.

'Where are we going, Tommy?'

'Cat burgling, have you got your torch?'

'Yep, it's up my sleeve.'

'Good lad, check the batteries, try it.'

I twist the end of it and it instantly lights up.

'Turn it off quick, I've just heard something. Stay still.'

It goes quiet for a minute.

'Right, let's go, wee man.'

'Where are we off to, Tommy?'

'Don't worry, just follow me, come on.'

We head across the grass towards an alleyway between two of the tenements, then over a couple of fences towards the shops. On the left of the shops, across a road and some steel railings, is what Tommy calls 'The Swag Factory'. It's actually Charleston School. We jump over the railings and look for a way in but all the doors and windows look pretty impossible to get in as we are only two tiny little people who think of ourselves as cat burglars, but we're hardly professionals.

Tommy has seen a massive tree branch on an old oak tree sticking over onto the school roof. 'Charlie, come here and I'll give ya a hiesty.'

He clasps his hands together, I put my foot on them, and he shoves me up the tree onto a low branch; then I pull him up a bit until he gets one hand hooked on and pulls himself up. He crawls along the branch above the roof to see if it's safe, drops onto the roof and I go next.

'Come on, wee man.'

When we're on the roof I'm thinking, *How the hell are we gonna get into the school from up here?*

Then a light bulb suddenly appears out of nowhere above Tommy's head and he's looking at these dome-shaped plastic things, which, I later find out, are roof vent lights.

His plan is simple. 'Charlie come 'ere. What we'll do is jump on these domes and see if they'll break, then we're in. I'll hold your arms. You stand on the dome and bounce up and down and if it breaks I'll have a hold on you so you won't fall into the classroom.'

'Good plan, Tommy,' I reply and stupidly begin climbing onto this plastic see-through death trap.

I bounce and bounce on this thing for about two minutes but it just isn't happening. It's making a lot of noise as well so Tommy pulls me back down off it.

'Let me try,' he says. 'Tommy, give me your arms.' As he climbs on he doesn't get the chance to grab my arms, the thing must have weakened from all my bouncing and with his extra weight he just disappears with an almighty crashing noise. I poke my head down and peer into the dark classroom through the hole we've just made – well, he has made.

'Tommy! Tommy! Are you alright?'

'Yeah, I've just got a bit of a dead arse.'

I start laughing nervously then as I know he's OK, but don't know if someone's heard us. You would have had to be pretty mutton Geoff not to hear that noise, or pretty pissed and used to loud bangs. Lucky we live in Scotland is all I can say. Tommy puts one desk on top of another desk and tells me to climb down. I climb into the dome and lower myself in, waiting for my feet to actually touch something. But being four feet high I'm never going to reach those desks even with a stepladder.

'Charlie, your feet are only about ten inches away from the desk, just drop down.'

I let go my hands really quickly. 'Holy shit,' I scream. It's more like another four feet to the desks and all I can feel is fresh air and then – *bang*, I slip sideways and Tommy catches me, pissing his sides laughing.

'It's the only way I could get you in, wee man. You would have bottled it if I'd told you the real height.'

'Yeah thanks for that, arsehole.'

'OK, I'll take one side of the corridor,' he says. 'You take the other.'

We take off around the school, trying doors and cupboards looking for the loot. I don't have a clue what we're looking for but Tommy's the man and we're on a job together – that's all I care about. In the back of my mind I'm thinking if we get caught I'll never be able to see Tommy again and then I'll be taken home to Dad and he hates police and if I bring them to the door then it might be curtains for me.

Tommy's gone on ahead into a room at the end of the corridor. It's the last door he's tried on his side of the building.

'Charlie,' he calls out, 'look at this, you fucking beauty.'

He comes out of the room with a massive biscuit tin in his hands. I can't believe he's getting that excited over biscuits – I mean, I like biscuits but he's taking it a wee bit too far.

'Big deal, you found some biscuits. Pocket some and let's get out of here.'

'It's no biscuits, you tube, it's money.'

'Let's see. Wow!'

I stare inside the tin. It looks just like treasure. I've never seen so many coins in one box. I feel like a pirate out with his first mate. Tommy puts the lid back on and we climb back up to the roof via the piled up desks and back down the tree, not dropping a single penny. We run back over the grass behind the tenements, up onto the bin shelter and back in the window that little Bobby has left open for us. We manage to sneak back into the house undetected.

*   *   *

The next morning we're out of the house at 8 a.m., not the norm for us on a Saturday but we have to get the treasure chest out of Mum's house. We walk around to the shops which are five minutes from the house. They're run down if not derelict – well, only one of the four shops on the row isn't boarded up and that one has steel grates over the whole shop front and concrete bollards cemented into the ground so cars can't ram-raid it. It's the Spar shop, the only one to survive. I think that's down to the fact that it's more secure than Fort Knox. Even the cameras have cameras.

I stay outside with the biscuit tin in a carrier bag while Tommy goes into the shop. He's taken some money in to buy sweets and bars of chocolate. He comes back out and we start munching Aeros, Mars bars, Marathons, etc. Soon I'm feeling as sick as a parrot, but Tommy's like a human dustbin, I've never seen anyone eat so much chocolate. All Tommy's friends turn up at the shops around 8.45 and we show them the loot. We buy nearly every child in Charleston a bag full of chocolate bars. We're a right couple of Robin Hoods, or, as my mum and the police put it, thieving little bastards.

Yes of course – we get captured.

As Tommy, fifty other kids and myself stand at the shops on the brink of vomiting from all the sugar, a hand tightly grabs the top of my arm – the arm carrying the treasure chest. I turn slowly and to my horror it's a copper and across the road, marching towards us with her sleeves rolled up, is Mum, not looking impressed one bit. I look at Tommy and he puts his finger up to his lips on the sly. I know exactly what he means: let him do the talking and agree with everything he says.

We stand against the wall while the police are talking to Mum. They're talking for ages, and I'm thinking, if I run now I'll make it back to St Mary's, but then my dad will find out so I'll have to stay and face the music. The police get back in the car and Mum walks towards us. You can see her blood is turning purple underneath. She doesn't even look like herself.

'Shift, you pair of idiots,' she hisses.

Oh God, I hope Mum is not as bad as Dad, I think. I'm suddenly very scared but Tommy puts his hand on my shoulder.

'Don't worry, wee man,' he whispers. 'It'll only last two minutes at the most.'

We get upstairs into the house and Mum sends us to the bedroom.

'Get in there now and lie on the bed face down.'

What the hell is gonna happen now? I think. Whatever Tommy says, I'm getting more terrified by the second.

Me and Tommy are now lying face down next to each other.

'What are you smiling for?' I say.

'Wait and you'll see, Charlie boy. Wait and see.'

Mum comes back into the room with this pink cotton belt off her jacket and gives us five each, then leaves the room and tells us to get out of her sight. I hardly feel a thing.

135

Tommy's been telling the truth: it has only lasted two minutes and the relief I'm feeling is ridiculous. I can't believe my luck: when I don't do anything I nearly get killed and when I do cause mayhem and steal I hardly get touched. What a crazy world. I just pray that Mum will never tell Dad.

I go back home to Dad on the Sunday. Mum drops me off at five in the evening.

'I'll see you next week when you come up here,' I tell Tommy.

'No you won't,' says Mum firmly. 'You can't see each other next week for what you've both done.'

I think that's fair enough as she hasn't told Dad, but I'm still gutted, to say the least. It means I've got another two weeks of purgatory to get through with Dad, counting down the days until I can see Tommy again. I never thought I'd feel like this about him, and never has my sentence at home with Dad seemed to drag on longer as the seconds and minutes tick by, and all the time I know that at any moment the beatings will start up again and my purgatory will turn once more to hell.

Chapter Thirteen

The Best Blanket in Dundee

It's eight in the evening and I'm watching TV. I've had my bath for school, all my homework's done, and I'm still thinking about what happened the day before, glad that the nutcase doesn't have a clue what I've been up to.

'I'm nipping to the shops.'

'OK, Dad.'

'Make sure you brush your teeth before I get back.'

'OK, Dad I will.'

The front door slams. I can tell he hates me spending time with Mum, probably in case I tell her what he's been doing to me. He's off to get his bottle of kick the dog – or vodka as other people know it. I haven't seen Bonnie all weekend and when I got home earlier she was jumping all over me as I came in the door. I could tell that he'd been hitting her, as there were little trails of wet patches on my bedroom floor where she had pissed herself with fear. I hate leaving her but Dad won't let me take her to Mum's as he'll have nobody to kick the shit out of.

He comes home fifteen minutes later, as he's had to walk because he's been banned from driving until about the year 3000 due to constant drink driving and crashes. He doesn't care though because every time they threaten to jail him the social work department and his legal-aid lawyer will play the single-parent stress card – and where would I go if he went to jail?

Put me in jail, I'll do the time as long as Bonnie can come with me.

The door opens. 'Have yi brushed yir teeth?'

'Yep,' I say brandishing my nashers. He sits in his chair next to the fire.

'Go an' get me a tumbler, the long one, not the whisky one.'

I know exactly which one he means – I've seen it a million times. I hop up off the couch in my Paisley pattern pyjamas and holly socks and go to get his glass.

'Get yirself a glass and I'll give yi some Coke.'

Yes! A treat. He's being all right with me. 'OK.'

I come back in, sit down and watch some party political programme with him. I never have a clue what these men in suits are going on about but Dad seems to think he's in the studio with them. He shouts stuff at one of the suits who's wittering on and says things like, 'You fucking tell the Tory bastard' and 'What have yi got to say aboot that, yi back-peddling bastards – answer the fucking question.'

Then he'll turn to me. 'Did you see that twat? I fucking hate people that answer a question with a question.'

I just agree and say, 'Yeah, why did he no' just answer him, Dad?'

'Because, Charlie, he's a right honourable wanker.'

For years to come I find myself calling the people who live in the TV the same thing, especially when I'm watching football. It's just one of many bizarre sayings that Dad comes out with. Another one is 'That Maggie Thatcher's got a puss like a welder's bench.' I always think she's got a lot of cramps in her face.

It's now about 11.30 at night and I'm getting a bit tired but I never dare ask if I can go to bed. I wait until he says, 'Go to yir bed' or he falls asleep, as I've learnt over the years that if I ask to go to bed the next line will be, 'Is there something up with my company, you ungrateful cunt. I let you stay up and that's the thanks I get.'

I can read him like a book eighty per cent of the time. He's now getting to that wobbly drink stage, when he suddenly turns around and looks at me, one eye straight and staring, the other looking towards his crooked nose.

'What did you tell yir mum the day,' slurring his words, sitting on the edge of his chair facing the telly but looking sideways at me with his elbows on his knees, all his fingers clasped together.

'Nothing, Dad, I never really seen her over the weekend. Me and Tommy were out playing all weekend.'

'*Fucking liar*, what are yi?'

'I'm not lying, Dad.'

'*Shut* the fuck up, liar, you speak when I tell you to speak. Did you hear me?'

'Yeah.'

'Only speak when I tell you to speak.'

I don't say another word as he lifts his vodka glass towards his mouth. He looks like a warped life-size version of a character in *Thunderbirds*, his body and arms and head bobbing and shifting like somebody's controlling them with strings. Then he puts the drink back down.

'What's this shit we're watching?' He can't even see the TV and right before my eyes he seems to be switching from one character to another. He's like a cross between the drunken, swearing Father Jack from *Father Ted* and Parker from *Thunderbirds*.

'Change the fucking channel, you liar. Where's my Coke, have you drunk all my fucking Coke?' Then he's mumbling, 'Greedy bastard, what a greedy bastard.'

His head is starting to dip towards his knees, swaying a little from side to side, then all of a sudden it shoots up and he'll stare sideways at me.

'I thought I told you to change the channel.'

Then he dips his head back down again and mumbles some more.

I watch him for about an hour and a half, waiting for him to fall asleep so I can get to bed, but every time I move, his head comes back up. He leans his cheek on his right hand, and takes a swig every ten or fifteen minutes. I look over to the corner and see Bonnie looking at me, not taking her eyes off me, waiting on me to go to bed so she can come with me. That dog is terrified of Dad, but she never leaves me alone with him when he's that drunk. It's like maybe she's got a plan to maul him, knowing that he won't remember. I swear that dog is brighter than a lot of humans I know.

I finally go to bed about four in the morning after I've waited to make absolutely sure that he's asleep, and Bonnie jumps on my bed before I get in. I turn all the lights off in the house but leave the fire on deliberately in the hope that Dad will roll over during the night and pull it on top of himself. But it never happens – not when I try to make it happen, that is.

He does manage to do it to himself once, though. I'm lying in bed one night asleep and I hear an almighty scream, which wakes me up. The fire in the living room is an electric two-bar fire with a metal grid over the front to stop you touching these red-hot heating rods; Dad has taken the grid off to light his roll-ups on it. He forgets to put it back on and falls asleep drunk on the floor with a pair of skin-tight green football shorts on that look more like women's hot pants.

Well, they soon become hot pants, as he rolls over in the night and burns two massive lines through his shorts and his arse cheek. I'm under the covers with my hand over my mouth as I'm never that good at holding in my laughter. Even Bonnie doesn't bark – I think she actually knows what's happened as well.

Bonnie's not just my best friend, my comforter and my constant companion. Through the bleak, bitter Dundee winter nights she's the best blanket you could imagine. Having a long-haired German Shepherd that sleeps over you is like having a radiator attached to your legs and a bodyguard all in one.

Bonnie's the thing that keeps me going, wanting to live, wanting to believe there must be a way out.

Chapter Fourteen

Air Vent

Living in St Fillans Road has been nothing short of a nightmare for me as a kid. I'm now aged ten and in the few short years I have lived there I have seen two of my friends being run over – one of them was Robbie, my cousin Shane's best friend. I've witnessed two people on separate occasions jump out of the Ardler seventeen-storey block of flats, their mangled bodies splattered only ten feet from where I was standing.

The second one was a woman in her fifties who jumped out of her fifteenth-floor window. When she hit the floor her foot (with the slipper still on) landed right next to me, and the fire crew and ambulance men had to scrape her off the road with a shovel while I stood and watched.

Things like that stick in your mind as a kid, and add to many sleepless nights because of the nightmares.

My nightmares are sometimes so horrific that I will force myself to stay awake, dreading going to sleep. Some nights I even think it's better to risk the torments of the living-room couch than to go to sleep. Most of the time, though, my living nightmare life with Dad is worse – and his behaviour can be even more unpredictable than my nightmares.

Seeing that woman on the floor makes me think, *Why did she jump? Was her husband torturing her? Did some evil bastard like Dad drive her to her death, as I've felt like doing for years?* The other person that jumped – well, there were actually loads that jumped – but the other one that I saw was a lad of twenty who had taken one too many drugs and thought he could fly. And same as my hamster, he definitely couldn't.

It's the noise more than anything that knocks me sick; the thud of a body hitting concrete is terrifying. I'm standing staring at his face squashed into the ground with a slight smile on it, thinking about how relaxed he looks. The police and firemen are trying to move all the screaming kids back, but I just stand there smiling back at him, and staring at how happy his face looks.

I hear a voice say, 'Get that kid away, he's in shock.'

I'm not in shock, I'm happy for him that his nightmare is over. I just wish to God mine could be too.

It's strange, as everything and everyone around me seems either to die or have bad things happen to them and I think it's only a matter of time before me and Bonnie go the same way, as I've been close to death a few times – obviously because of Psycho Dad. And my own stupidity doesn't help either, with the places I explore.

One day I'm in a car park between the first two multi-storey blocks of flats – the seventeen-storey ones. There's a top level and a bottom level and in the latter there's an air vent kind of heating system, with silver boxlike vents that go all around the roof space of the car park. There's a few access points with steel covers on the front so that you can climb up and crawl around the vents.

We take candles up because it's pitch black and leave them for the next people that come. On this particular day I'm with my mate Calum Patterson, my old partner in crime. I climb into the vent first and light a candle, and Calum comes up behind me. I'm five yards in from him and can smell something in the vent. It's the same smell as the night Bonnie got her nosed rubbed in her own shit, and it seems to get stronger as I crawl along.

'Charlie?'

'What, Calum?'

'Have you stood in shite?'

'No, Calum, I just forgot to brush my teeth this morning.'

'If your breath smelt like that I'd seriously consider going to the dentist.'

'Ha! ha! … *Ahhh!*' I let out an almighty roar.

'What is it, Charlie?'

'Go back! Go back! I've just touched something' fuckin' hairy.'

'What are you doing in here, Mum?' Calum shouts.

This breaks me up. After I've got over my fit of laughter, I'm still trying to get that nutter to reverse as there isn't enough room in the vent to turn around. It's only about two foot square.

'Go back, Calum, go back, I think it's dead rats.'

'It's not the rats you wanna be scared of, it's whatever killed them that worries me.'

'Shut yir puss Calum and reverse.'

Well, the next thing I know, this roaring sound bellows up the vent.

'What the fuck is that?' Calum screams. The roar is deafening and we're being sucked towards this massive thing that looks like an aeroplane propeller. It's actually pulling us towards it. We never realised that this air vent thing actually works. We're facing the wrong way, and can't really see what's going on behind us and the noise is deafening. Then the rat I put my hand on earlier comes scraping down the side of my face.

That is it, I'm outta here – I am officially going to touch cloth. I hear a clang and clatter behind me and think, shit, Calum's been chopped up into mincemeat and I'm next.

Suddenly I find myself falling, banging off both sides of the vent shaft we climbed up at the beginning.

'Fuck me, that was close,' says Calum, when we finally get our breath. His ginger hair's standing up all over the place, like he's just been electrocuted.

'Do you want to go back in, Calum?' I laugh.

'You can fuck right off, you lunatic. I thought the party wiz over then,' he admits.

Calum still looks like a kid, but he speaks and acts like a man. We'll walk into the shops to get crisps or juice or something and he'll pay for his and say to the eighteen-year-old Asian girl, 'Cheers, Mary doll, keep the ten pee change and phone yir mum to tell ir yir commin' ti meh hoose fir tea.'

You'd think he was forty years old.

You can never beat him in a slanging match either. Whatever you say to him he has fifteen better answers to chuck back at you. Most of the sayings I grow up with come from him, like 'When you were young, did your mum and dad feed you with a catapult?'

Although I had Calum, Shane and Tommy, Bonnie is still – and will always be – the very best friend I've ever had. Even though she's a huge long-haired German Shepherd with teeth like a wolf, she's a really friendly dog, especially with kids. We'd roll about the floor play-fighting together for hours. I grab her in a head lock and pretend to bite her ear, making a playful, snarling noise, then she wriggles out of it and pins my arms down with her paws, puts her massive, powerful jaw around my neck and makes the same noise back. This game can last for hours. We crawl around on all fours, taking each other's legs away, but she always treats me the same way a lion mother treats a new-born cub. We trust each other one hundred per cent.

But on one occasion Bonnie's not in the mood for playtime, as my brown Y-fronts soon realise. Tommy is over, staying for the weekend at Dad's, and Bonnie's in season again. She's always grumpy with people at times like this, but hey, what woman isn't! When Bonnie's like this I seem to be the only person who can go near her – well, until this particular morning. Tommy and I go downstairs to the kitchen for breakfast, passing Bonnie in the living room. I pat her head as I walk past in my underpants and she seems fine as she wags her tail. After breakfast she jumps up to start our morning play ritual – as I often do, I turn so that my back is to her, and then walk backwards towards her. That way, she can't get my hands.

As I back her into the corner with my backside, Tommy's laughing and says, 'She's gonna bite your arse one o' these days!'

All of a sudden, before I can say 'No, she won't,' I feel her teeth grab my left butt cheek as she's now pushing me out of the corner and across the room.

She never breaks the skin though and I will always believe ever after that she understood what Tommy had said, and that she actually has a human sense of humour.

Tommy and I carry on seeing each other at weekends, one weekend at Mum's the next at Dad's. We even have a few good times with Dad, like when we go to Glenshee for a week's skiing and there isn't any snow so we have to go up the dry ski slopes. We have these big massive skis with rollers on them, like rollerblades. We're at the top of this hill and Tommy goes flying down it.

'Look at me, Dad,' he turns and shouts, 'look at me,' and as he's shouting, he smashes his forehead straight into a barrier and his feet go halfway around it.

Another time, Dad has this big coat on and slides on a hill and everyone's pelting him with snowballs.

Dad's still football manager for Dundee West. He manages the older kids, Tommy's age, and plays me a couple of times for the team but I'm really too small – paper thin. One day Dundee West go to play against Arbroath, a town up the east coast, twenty minutes from Dundee – and the Dundee kids can't believe their eyes: all these hulking great fourteen-year-old Arbroath kids have beards! Most of the time fifteen or twenty kids come back to our house and have a bath and if they haven't let in more than ten goals Dad gives them all a Mars bar, because they're all basically crap!

One of the bravest things I've ever done is when Tommy's over to see me one weekend. Dad's falling about pissed and finally jumps in the shower. Meanwhile I'm looking for my stick insect. I normally keep it in a jar but it's managed to get out and could be anywhere by now. I'm looking all over the carpet and up the walls but finally give up and sit and watch TV with Tommy.

Suddenly the door opens – Dad's come out of the bath-room and his towel falls off.

'There it is,' I say, pointing at his willy. 'I've found it, Dad!'

Fortunately, for once Dad sees the funny side and laughs – but mainly, I'm thinking, because Tommy's there.

Dad still works as a roofer and one day he takes me and Tommy with him, along with his friend Hatchy. He's replacing some roof tiles on a house in a rich area of Dundee called Broughty Ferry and we have to hand the tiles up to him. Dad's up on the roof, Tommy's at the top of the ladder while I'm running up and down the ladder with the tiles and Hatchy's standing at the bottom.

'Tell her I need some water!' Dad shouts down to Hatchy.

Now Hatchy's a really nice guy but he's a wee shy. So I accompany him as he nervously goes to ask the owner of the house, a middle-aged woman, for the water.

'Would you like it hot or cold?' she says in this posh voice.

'Jock, the woman wants to know if yi want it hot or cold!'

When Dad calls back down, Hatchy's face goes as red as beetroot.

'Hot!' says Dad. 'And wi' a fuckin' teabag in it.'

Chapter Fifteen

Bonnie and Me under the Stars

Dad has been waiting on a new house for a few years, a semi-detached from the council is what he's always dreamed about. The tenements are good in the sense that all the kids know each other and hang around together and most people can leave their doors open and wander in and out of each other's houses. Ours are locked because Dad doesn't want anyone walking in while he's wasting me or the dog.

When I'm ten years old, his wish comes true. I don't know how he manages it but he wangles a three-bedroom semi in St Nicholas Place, a nice street about a quarter of a mile to the north of St Fillans Road with a lot of semi-detached houses both sides of the street. They have big back gardens and a play park at the bottom of the road with swings and a roundabout and the public works shed in the middle. There's also a big grass area around the park and a barracks where a few years later, at the age of thirteen, I end up going to the cadets. It's only three streets over from St Fillans Road but it's a lot nicer than the house we've been living in.

I can't wait to move out of that house in St Fillans Road. It has so many bad memories for me, and the new house could mean a new start. At the very least it's a new adventure and maybe soon I'll have the strength and size to kill that drunken bastard. Those are the thoughts that are creeping around in my head, and I think Bonnie's thinking the same. As she's now fully grown and has teeth like a wolf, I'm just glad she's on my side.

We move to St Nicholas Place in the summer of 1986. It's the school holidays and we have to move all the tat that Dad has collected over the years from St Fillans Road into our new place. Some of Dad's drinking buddies help us move in.

It doesn't take long for us to get settled. We decorate with the grant that the social has given Dad. He builds a big long two-foot-high fire surround that goes around three walls and has pre-varnished pine tongue-and-groove around the face of it. It's a long living room with a window at each end, and he's put wallboards on the other two walls – don't ask me why, I think that must be the fashion. It's like living in a log cabin the amount of wood in there.

The back garden's a bonus for Bonnie as she loves to play around in it – and we can also let her out to do her business.

The kitchen is off the living room, and the stairs go up to three bedrooms and a bathroom. This is the first time I've lived in a house with a staircase *inside* it; in the old place stairs meant piss and graffiti.

We must be going up in the world, I think to myself.

Dad still has a car, which I find a bit confusing as he's been banned from driving for the next 3000 years. I don't think he ever did pass his test, or even own a provisional licence; he has his own rules and laws, ones that are different to anyone I've ever known.

The car is an old orange Vauxhall Cavalier with thirty dents in it where Dad has been playing dodgems on the way back from the pub over the years. The driver's seat is covered in cigarette burns and the ashtray is overflowing with butts as he keeps them in case of emergencies. He breaks them all up into a cigarette paper and makes his own, which I actually think is pretty clever.

The car's covered in dog hairs as well, as Bonnie regularly moults twice a year. We take her to Clatto Park, which I told you about earlier, where the swans live on the two islands in the middle of this big reservoir.

Dad will throw a stick into the water so that Bonnie will swim out and get it. I think he's trying to wind the swans up or get Bonnie to bring one back so we can have swan butties. Don't panic – she never catches one!

Then when we're on the way home Bonnie jumps on the back seat and covers it in wet fur. The smell of wet dog is stomach churning and I can never get used to it. It's a bit like the old man in the post office that so kindly emptied the contents of his bowels in my face.

As a kid Clatto Park is my idea of heaven. It's in the middle of some woods at the back of St Mary's, about a five-minute drive from my new house. It has a mini manmade beach with boats, canoes and wind surfing. There's loads of pike and perch in there as well; it has fishing competitions a few times a year. The actual reservoir is surrounded by sloping stones that lead up to a walking path all the way around the top so you can look down on the water. It's a bit like a First Division football club, where the pitch is the water and the small sloping terraces are the stone areas.

There's also one of those zip slides which I love playing on – you stand on a round disc connected to a long bar that you hold on to, then slide down a steel cable and crash into a tyre at the bottom. It's the tyre that softens the impact when you come to a sudden halt. All around the park are barbecues and benches for sitting on in the summer. You can hire wet suits and life-jackets as well if you've got the money, but most people end up jumping in with just a pair of shorts on, then peeling the leaches off when they get back out.

Even though the park is brilliant and has a lot going on, a more interesting place for me is a field at the back of Clatto. Dad sends me up there sometimes with a couple of carrier bags and tells me to fill them and come straight back home. But it's not an ordinary field. It belongs to a huge, scary farmer called Big Ged who has a double-barrelled shot-gun and permission to have a pop at anyone on his land or property.

In between Clatto Park and his field there are pine trees thirty feet tall which are all very close together. The back of Clatto has everything – spuds, veg plots and rabbits, if you can catch them – and the woods are so tightly compact that even the Scottish rain finds it nearly impossible to break through onto the forest floor. It's always dark going through them even during the day, but it's worth clambering through the woods because at the other side in the field are potatoes. And not just any potatoes – these are called Kerr's Pinks.

They're about five times the size of a normal spud and as pink as a pig's snout. They taste brilliant, even raw, if you've run away from home and need food, although running away from home is not something I would ever dare do because I'm too scared of what would happen if I got caught and was then sent back to Dad. The consequences and his reprisals don't bear thinking about.

But then again, as David Bowie might have said about Bonnie and me, we could be heroes just for one day. And there is one single night when we do get away – our night of freedom together.

It's two in the morning, Dad is snoring at the fire, paralyt-ically drunk. I take Bonnie, sneak out of the back door and head up to Clatto.

The Nipper

We sit on the jetty, where the boats are tied up. I sit with my arm around Bonnie, washing the blood from my face with my free hand. It's great to breathe the crisp fresh air into my lungs, as the smoke-filled room I'm used to makes it hard to breathe normally.

I lie back with my head on Bonnie, looking at the stars through the dark night, thinking of what life is going to bring, and wondering whether I'll be able to survive much longer.

I can hear fish jumping in the dark and an owl hooting in the woods behind me. I'm scared about going into the woods but I have to get to the potato field as I remember the spuds taste so juicy.

I picked a huge one and scoff the whole thing as I walk around the reservoir, throwing a stick in the water for Bonnie. She runs and belly flops in, just like a human, then comes back to me and shakes herself all over me.

It's brilliant tonight – we're free for a few hours, Bonnie and me, to do what we want. I take Bonnie back to the jetty and fall asleep next to her until the sun breaks through the morning sky.

We rush home and sneak back in, petrified about being caught but it's fine. We're both back in our prison and Dad's still in the same position as last night and I never do get caught for my night of freedom.

Even so, I wish every night could be like this one.

* * *

The first time I meet Big Ged the farmer is the last time I ever taste Kerr's Pink spuds, as it's the last time I ever set foot in his field. It's around six o'clock in the evening on a warm summer Sunday night and it's still very bright out in the open. Me and Calum Patterson are up at Clatto catching bees in jam jars and watching a couple of older blokes fishing.

'Caught anything, mate?' Calum asks one of the fishermen.

'A couple o' perch. I had a massive pike on but it snapped the line.'

Calum puts his hand up to his mouth. 'Bullshit!' he says, faking a cough.

'What did you say, yi little dick?'

'Nothing mate, I've got a bad cough.'

I start laughing at Calum. He's always trying to wind people up.

'What size were the pike's teeth, mate?' he says in an innocent tone.

'They were huge like!'

'Was it like *Jaws*?'

I'm already trying not to laugh because I know what Calum's doing.

'I'll crack your puss, yi wee fanny.'

'You'll have to catch me first, mate.'

'Keep winding me up, ginger.'

'What are ya gonna dae, set one o' yir sharks on me?'

'Right, you little fucker.'

Calum takes to his heels into the woods and the bloke drops his fishing rod and chases after him. I'm pissing my sides as Calum's now running and shouting, 'Kin yi no tak a joke!! I wiz only joking.'

The bloke is actually winding Calum up, as he winks when he runs past me, but I don't let on as I want to see how far Calum will run. Finally the bloke comes walking back without Calum as he's too tall to get through all the low branches that Calum glides under with no problem.

'See ya lads, good luck,' I say.

'Yea, see ya wee man.'

I head off into the trees in the direction of Big Ged's field, shouting at the top of my voice, 'Calum it's me, Calum where are yi?'

'Charlie! Ahhgh you scared the shit out of me then.'

He's up a tree four feet from my head and screaming my name in the pitch black. He gets down from the tree and we can see light poking through the bottom of the branches.

'This wiy, Calum. Come on.'

'This is no the wiy oot.'

'I know, we're going to Big Ged's field.'

'No chance, Charlie, he blows people's fucking heads off.'

'No he doesn't, I've nicked aboot forty bags o' his tatties and I've still got a head!'

'You could do with a new one.'

'Shut it, carrot top.'

'OK, Plug.'

I'm not going to get into a slagging match with him as I haven't won one yet. Oh yeah! My ears stick out – hence the plug comment.

'Shut up, Calum, are you coming or are you a pussy?'

'Give me a bowl of milk and I'll tell you.' He's very hard to have a serious conversation with.

'OK then, clever arse, I'll go and get some free tatties and you head back to that lad that wants to put you on the end of his hook and I don't mean his fishing hook.'

'What hook do ya mean?'

'A fuckin' left hook – dowball, come on.'

We start walking towards the field. Calum has decided to come with me as it's a bit safer – well, as far as he knows.

'Charlie!'

'Yeah, what is it?'

'If Farmer Ged blows your legs off, don't come running to me!'

'Shut up, you half-wit,' I giggle.

We climb over the barbed-wire fence that surrounds the field and go on our mission. Calum is looking a bit edgy, sticking close behind me and peering all around like a meerkat on its back legs.

'If I hear a bang I'm oot o' here.'

'If you hear a bang, Calum, ane o' us will be horizontal.'

'Shut it, Charlie, I'm already turtling.' He means he's shitting himself.

159

We have to walk quite a bit into the field as the side next to the woods has been plundered by the whole of St Mary's. Nobody ever goes more than halfway across as the fear of becoming target practice is too much. Not me though, I've coped with a lot more than a little double-barrelled shotgun in my life. At least in a field you have the chance of escape.

'Right, Calum boy, this will do here. Get digging.'

'I've not got a shovel.'

'With your hands, yi dork.'

'Alright, there's no need to get personal.'

I can't even look at him without laughing. Every time he opens his mouth I can feel my cheekbones against the bottom of my eyes.

'Charlie!'

'Yeah, what is it?'

'Is there a point to what we're dain' here?'

'Of course, mate, we're on a mission.'

It isn't just that. I'm trying to score some brownie points with Dad and I knew Calum wasn't arsed about the spuds so I'd have double the amount to take home.

'I think we have enough now, Charlie.'

I turn around and he has twenty or so great big spuds cradled in his pulled-up jumper, and behind him is this massive figure that reminds me of a silverback gorilla.

It's Big Ged. He looks like a cross between the Jolly Green Giant and Quasimodo. He has a brown cap on, a grey, hand-knitted jumper with holes in it, and a shotgun leaning on his shoulder pointing up towards the sky.

We both just freeze, as there's no chance of escape with one of those things being fired at you. Calum lets go of his jumper and all the spuds land at his feet. I just keep staring at the gun, hoping he won't lower it in my direction.

'It was his idea, mister,' Calum pipes up. 'I dinna even eat tatties.'

Big Ged just keeps standing there staring at me with his big black beadie eyes. His pupils are massive – you can't see the actual colour of his eyes, but they look a bit like great big shiny balls of chocolate, like Minstrels.

'Have you got anything to say, thief?'

That's Ged's first words as he looks at me.

'We're homeless, mister,' I say quickly. 'We got kicked out of the home we lived in, and we've not eaten for days.'

His angry expression instantly changes – I think he's looking sorry for us, even saddened. I've got him hook, line and sinker and I'm just praying that Calum doesn't open his gob and ruin the story I've made up.

I've become a brilliant liar, as I've had to tell so many for Dad over the years.

'Pick them tatties back up,' says Big Ged, as he turns to Calum.

Calum looks confused and looks to me.

'Go on then, it's alright,' I say.

The farmer turns back to me. 'I'll never see you in this field again, will I?'

'No I promise, mister, you'll never see me again.'

'Right, get lost!'

'Thanks, mister.'

'Yeah, cheers mister,' Calum pipes in.

It's funny you know, everybody had said for years that Big Ged the farmer was evil, but I've seen a different man than what I believed him to be. And even though I've been telling him what he wanted to hear so he wouldn't fill the both of us with shotgun pellets, I never do go back near his field again. As for Big Ged, those thirty odd tatties he's given us have bought him two less people stealing his livelihood.

We walk back across the field towards the woods and Calum keeps looking back behind him, as he never believes we're gonna get off that easy.

'I'll bet yi a tennar that nutter shoots us when wir at the fence.'

'Just keep walkin', Calum. Everything's cool.'

We climb the fence and walk through the woods back towards the reservoir.

'Shit!' Calum stops. 'What aboot that guy that wiz fishin' earlier, you go up and check if he's there.'

'He was only winding you up mate, he wisna really gonna do ya.'

'Oh! Does he think he's funny? I'd fuckin' take him one on one anyway.'

He never does learn. Just out of one situation and he wants to go and start another load of hassle.

'You don't have to prove to him, Calum. Eh ken you can do him, and you ken yi kid do him, so dinna worrie aboot it.'

'*Exactamungo*, me old flower.'

Where the hell does he get all these sayings?

We head back through Clatto towards home, the lads that were fishing earlier have moved away round the other side and it's getting a bit dark.

'I'd better get home, Calum, I'm starvin'.'

'Yeah me tae, I could eat a scabby horse.'

I think he means he's hungry. We head back into St Mary's down towards my house, as he lives further down at the bottom of St Fillans Road. We reach my house, and Calum empties the contents of his jumper onto my next-door neighbour's car boot.

'I'll see yi in the morin', mate.'

'Yeah, I'll come doon fir yi when I get up. See yi, mate.'

I run into the house through the side door leading into the kitchen to get a carrier bag for the spuds. I can't wait to see what Dad will say. Just for once he's going to be pleased with me. And now that we've moved to St Nicks, everything could be different between us.

It really could be a new start.

Chapter Sixteen

Home Sweet Home

'Is that you, Charlie?'

'Yeah it's me, Dad. I'll just be a minute.'

I run back out to the car, fill the bag and run back in, then close the side door.

'What the fuck are yi dain?'

I open the kitchen door into the living room. 'Look, Dad, spuds.'

'Where did yi git them?'

'At the back o' Clatto – Kerr's Pinks!'

I'm now standing with a massive smile on my face, waiting for an equally massive pat on the back.

'What did I tell about thieving?'

Nothing, I think. *I've done it with you before*.

'I've got them with you before, Dad – at the back o' Clatto.'

'Did I say yi could nick tatties fae Clatto?'

'No, Dad, but I thought—'

'Oh, yi thought, did yi?'

He doesn't look that drunk, but he's had a few.

'Sit doon, geeze that fucking bag!' He snatches it out of my hand. 'Are yi awa ti start yir shit up here now?' He means the new house and area in St Nicholas Place. 'Next it'll be the polis at the door.'

You've got some neck, I think, you're on first-name terms with every copper in Scotland.

'And I just thought—'

'Yeah, yi said that earlier.'

Let me speak, you evil bastard. That's what I feel like saying.

'I tried to save you money.' I've actually managed to rattle a sentence off without being interrupted.

'Are yi tryin' to say eh canna afford tatties like? Is that yir brilliant excuse, is it? Eh canna afford tatties!' he shouts at me. 'Well, OK yi better go and cook them then. Oh I forgot, yiv never peeled a fucking tattie in yir life.'

I've been making stuff to eat for myself while you've been comatose since I was six, I think angrily to myself.

He throws the bag of spuds in my direction, then takes a swig from his glass. 'What else did yi git up ti the day? Rob any grannies, smash some phone boxes, did yi have a good time, while I've been lookin after *yir dog!*'

'But Dad, you—'

165

'*But Dad, but Dad, but Dad* …' he mocks in a high-pitched voice. 'If I had a pound for every time yi said "but Dad", yi wouldna have to go and stale tatties. "But Dad this, but Dad I'm sorry, but Dad, it wasn't my fault" … *Fuck yi* we yir "but dads". I'm no yir dad.'

He stands up and walks towards me, 'Yir uncle's yir dad and fae now on yi say, "But Mug", my new name is Mug, no Dad, Mug.'

I feel like going into the kitchen, grabbing a knife and driving it right through his pissed up, crooked, evil face. Even though I'm shit scared I'm getting angry and he detects it in my face.

'Oh di yi no like Daddy saying that,' he says, mock slapping me in the face and talking to me in a baby voice as if I were three years old. 'Yi'll never be big enough, yi little shit.'

Then a punch comes out of nowhere, and rattles the side of my jaw. I've forgotten how hard his punch can be, as he has been legless for the past couple of years when he's battered me, and he's only tipsy now. I fall sideways onto the couch and the white flash I see is weird – it's the same flash you see when you get electrocuted.

He sits back down in his chair and takes another sip of his voddy. 'See what yi've made me do now, yi little cunt.'

Oh I'm sorry, did I hurt your hand with my jaw? I can taste the blood inside my mouth, as I've bitten my cheek on the inside when he smacked me, and I can feel one of my teeth has come loose and my jaw's throbbing.

'I'm sorry, Dad,' I say feebly.

'I'm no yir dad, are yi deaf?'

Another four inches higher with that punch and I would have been.

'You call me "Mug" fae now on.'

Yeah right, so you can do the Highland Fling on my nut again. No thanks, I think I'll pass.

He's trying to get me to call him a mug. I'm sure he enjoys me calling him names or swearing, so he can get more wound up. Not that he needs any help in that department.

Bonnie has taken off upstairs at the beginning, as even she knows that different levels of drunk mean different levels of memory the next day. If he's falling about trying to batter one of us Bonnie will stick around, because he misses with a lot of shots and she wants to keep an eye on me. She also knows that he'll forget the next day. But if he's this kind of drunk, she knows that he'll go back and forward from me to her, and the pain is sometimes too much for her to take.

I just sit there for the next hour and a half saying nothing, watching him drink then refill his glass with voddy and Coke. He doesn't speak to me either – it's another one of his mental torture games. Then he'll stand up really quick as if it's all going to kick off, and then stretch and sit back down, smirking at the fact that I've just flinched.

The twat enjoys it. It's taken me a long time to realise it – the whole of six years since I was four years old. Now I'm ten I'm starting to see it: he's trying to make me lose it. And it works. My mind is being overloaded with so many confusing things, I start thinking that I'm the one who's crazy and not him.

Around five hours have passed and I'm starving but I can't talk until he talks or it might start him off. My stomach's making rumbling noises, and I even try to muffle them with a cushion, as I don't want him to remember I'm still there.

'What are yi fuckin' sittin' there for?'

I don't answer.

He turns back towards the TV, swaying a bit now. '*I said*, what are yi fuckin' *lookin*' at me for?'

What! He never said that a minute ago, did he? I think I must be losing the plot.

'I'm just watchin' TV, Dad.'

'*My* TV, not yirs,' he says in a deep, slurred voice. 'That's a' yir good it, sitting there we yir miserable puss. Well what, what what do yi want me ti dae aboot it?' He's now talking in riddles. 'Blame yir mum, dinna blame me, blame the neighbours. Dinna blame me.'

What on earth are you talking about? I'm thinking.

'Blame Maggie Thatcher,' he shouts, swaying about in his chair. 'It's her fault we've no got a pot ti piss in.' He stands up, turns towards me with his hands out by his sides, kind of like he's on a cross. 'That's ma boy.' Then he tries to kick me in the face. He misses as I move to the side, but he falls sideways, landing on top of me. 'Oh good move, yi never seen that one coming, did yi?'

I obviously did, hence the fact you missed.

'Oh this is comfy.' He's now sitting on my head, squashing it into the couch. 'What aboot dead legs, do ya like them?' He starts punching me in the legs and ribs. 'Do ya like them, good, ald. Dead. Legs.'

He's punching me each time he says a word, and kind of singing as he does it. 'Do you like dead legs, baby?'

He then turns over and kneels on my face, crushing the side that he has smacked earlier. I am in agony, screaming, 'Dad stop, *stop Dad.*' But this only seems to make him more angry.

'Shut yir puss,' he says, taking his knee off my head and replacing it with his big nicotine-stained hand. He covers my mouth and nose and is now laying his full bodyweight on top of me. 'Shut yir puss, shut yir puss,' he whispers. It's so that the neighbours won't hear.

I'm struggling because I can't breathe and I feel like I'm going to pass out, but he just keeps moving his hand with my head from side to side. Then he lets go and starts laying into my face with both hands. One of my hands is stuck under my back and the other one is doing a crap job of blocking the blows. I can see the blood on his hands every time a punch comes and it's starting to splatter on his top.

He suddenly stops and pulls me onto the floor by the hair, dragging me around saying, 'Yi'll no stale tatties fae this hoose again.'

That's how messed up his head is – he's now persuaded himself that I've stolen the spuds from him. That's the last thing on my mind though. I just want to get away from him to catch a breath. He drags me over to the kitchen door and leans me against it. I'm covering my face as by now I can't stand any more: I've taken enough. My head is throbbing where he's pulled my hair out.

'Let is see yir face.' I keep my hands tight over my face.

'I'm no gonna hit ya, let is see yir face.'

He's standing leaning over me. I can smell his putrid breath and I can see through my hands that he has one hand on the doorframe above me and the other with a clump of my blood-soaked hair in it.

'Please dinna hit is again, Dad.'

'I'll no', let is see.'

I think he must be panicked with the sight of the blood so I move my hands away.

'Fuckin' hell,' he says. 'Was that me?'

He crouches down beside me and puts one arm on his knee, leaning so he won't fall over. He lifts his hand towards my face slowly, staring at me with the evil-looking squint in his eyes he gets when he's drunk.

'Fuckin' hell,' he says again as he touches my cheekbone. 'What a fuckin' mess, you'll hae a shiner the mor'in.'

Then out of the blue. *Poke!*

Aghhhgg! Another one of them flashes again. He's poked his index nicotine-stained finger straight into my eye.

Ahhgg, aghhgg. Then it starts again for another three hours.

170

He drags me from one side of the room to the other, stamping on my head and picking things up from the table to hit me with, stopping every ten minutes for another drink. I can safely say I've had a few close shaves in my life but this feels like the closest I have ever come to dying.

He eventually falls asleep on the floor next to the fire as usual and I crawl upstairs to my bedroom, stopping at the bathroom to clean myself up.

I hobble in and sit down on the toilet, pulling my sleeves up to check my arms as apart from my head they are the things that are aching the most. I can hardly see any of my skin colour for purple and blue bruises and there are lumps sticking out of my forearms and hands. I stand up and walk over to the sink to wash the blood from my hands and face as I can feel it still running off the end of my nose. I turn the tap on and then tilt a small square mirror down to have a look.

Oh my God. My face is covered in blood, both my eyes are three-quarters closed, my cheeks and eyebrows have open cuts with a little blood still trickling out of them and my lips are massive with dried blood on the inside. All this is horrible but I'm mesmerised by the sight of my hair.

I seem to have had an Eighties back comb, with a dark red Mohican up the middle. As I put my hands through it, clumps of hair fall out and my head looks like someone has lifted the scalp, inserted a load of golf balls and then sewed it back on. I give myself a quick once over with a wet cloth as I won't risk turning the bath taps on in case he wakes up again.

I stumble into my room and sit on the end of the bed, with Bonnie sitting between my legs, licking one of the cuts on the inside of my arm. I'm just sitting there tickling behind Bonnie's ears, thinking of what's just happened. I can see in her eyes that she's upset at the fact that she didn't come down to help me, but I'm glad it wasn't her.

The next morning I wake up with the bed sheet stuck to my face where all the blood from my open cuts has soaked into it. It's nine o'clock and I can see the sunlight shining through a gap in the curtains. My eyes are now almost fully closed and my top lip is pressing against the under-side of my nose. The worst thing though is my head: the areas that have had hair pulled out feel like a vice's being tightened on them. Every part of me is swollen, bruised or cut, but I'm just thankful that Bonnie never got touched. I always feel worse the next day if she's the one that gets hurt.

Dad has made some excuse to Mum why Tommy can't come over next weekend and that gives him a couple of weeks for me to recover; he cannot risk Mum finding out. She's already a bit suspicious after the time Dad took Tommy and me to watch Dundee United at Tannadice. Tommy was jumping around and Dad kept telling him to keep still and had his arms around him. I find out years later that when Tommy got back to Mum's that weekend she found bruises all over him and asked him where they came from.

'I was jumping around cheering and Dad was nipping me.'

Mum went ballistic. The following week social services came up to see if I was OK but I think they caught me on a day when Dad had just bought me some trainers or something. And the fact that I didn't want to die that young made me keep my mouth shut about what he was doing.

Tommy tries to take his revenge on Dad over the next couple of years though. They're more equally matched in strength and Tommy has always had much less fear of Dad than I've had. He hasn't been terrorised by him all these years and as far as he's concerned, Dad's just a nasty cunt who deserves a good hiding and it's only a matter of time before he'll get it, Tommy says.

The first time he fights back is when Dad's drunk and is trying to hit us both at the same time and Tommy manages to push Dad over the couch. Dad drags himself up from the floor and lurches around, trying to land a punch, but Tommy darts away and Dad's just too pissed to retaliate.

After another fight with him Dad whacks Tommy in the face with a Pod sandal and is about to start on me. Tommy jumps up in rage and pushes him over the couch and as Dad lands on the floor Tommy runs out of the house. Dad's trying to struggle back up to his feet, but he's so full of alcohol he can't make it.

'Don't listen to him,' we can hear him shouting. 'He's full of shit like his mum.'

'Come on, Charlie,' Tommy calls out to me outside in the street as I stand in the front doorway. 'Yi don't want to stay here with that fuckin' bastard. He's crazy! Let's go home to Mum's.'

But although Dad's too drunk to follow us, I'm now torn between following Tommy and my fear of Dad sobering up the next day and coming to get me. I can see a look that's between sadness and anger on Tommy's face and in the end I don't dare leave the house. And when Tommy sees the look in my eyes – of pure fear – he starts to realise what kind of reign of terror Dad's been subjecting me to all these years.

It hits him hard. In fact, he's mad as hell about it and it makes me realise something. Dad sometimes tells me that Granddad used to beat up his brother, Uncle Danny, as well as beating up Dad. It made Dad really mad to see his little brother getting hurt and when I see how wound up Tommy is about Dad beating me up I get a kind of new insight into why Tommy reacts that way. It's really a case of history repeating itself – except I still can't imagine Granddad ever subjected either of his boys to the vicious physical barrages and mental torture Dad has inflicted on me over the years.

If Mum knew even a fraction of what had gone on over the last six years, I can't imagine the consequences. But after years of keeping silent about my extended torture, it's become second nature to keep quiet – and, now that we're reunited, to keep it from Mum.

I'm too scared to say anything to her about it when I stay weekends, and she never asks me – not directly at least. But every time I see her, she says, 'Is everything OK at your dad's?'

'Yeah it's fine, Mum,' I always reply.

But I don't really need to say anything because ever since the night when Tommy tried to get me to leave with him, he's been telling Mum and Dale what he's guessed has been going on – he's worked it all out from Dad's habitual drunken, violent behaviour and from that scared look on my face. He only tells me about all this later and I still assume that Mum and Dale know nothing about how Dad treats me.

Then one weekend Dad goes to pick me up from Mum's and she keeps me upstairs.

'Wait a minute, son,' she says, 'yir dad's downstairs, but can yi give us a hand with this?'

It's a table by one of the beds she wants me to help her move and while I'm giving her a hand, Dale and Tommy go downstairs and Dale smashes Dad through the car window.

'I know what you did to Charlie,' he says and breaks his nose – and Tommy later tells me he's joined in and slapped and punched Dad.

Of course Dale doesn't really know a fraction of what Dad's been up to – and I haven't said anything. At first Dad says nothing when I return to him from Mum's. He's still nursing his broken nose and is quieter than usual, grumpy and morose, but at least he seems to lay off me for a while.

For a while ...

But then it starts up all over again and within a few weeks he's beating me with a vengeance, along with more interrogations.

'What did you tell them, yi little bastard?'

'Nothing, Dad. I didn't say anything.'

'So what did that fucker mean by "know what you did?" I suppose he got it from the fairies ... Or maybe it was Tommy, eh? Has he been telling lies about me?'

'No, Dad.'

'I don't believe you, you dirty little lying scumbag ...'

And on and on he goes.

In years to come I wish I had told Mum everything as she would have killed him before he got me. But even after Dale and Tommy beat Dad up, I remain silent. I don't want to have to tell her. Maybe she doesn't really want to know the whole truth, I say to myself, and besides, it would break her heart if she discovered everything I've been through all this time. Yet I'm sure she must suspect it. After all, she of all people should know what Dad's capable of, from the years of beatings she suffered at his hands.

Even so, I always believe that, if I say anything, Dad will slither his way out of it and then ... I will die.

No beatings, no more hours and hours of taunts and torture.

I will simply be killed.

Chapter Seventeen

Big Geoff and Wee Geoff

I think the thing that confuses me most about Dad is his two personalities. Sober, he's Funny Jock, who can be warm, generous and caring; but drunk he can turn in a flash into Evil Jock, an animal that doesn't even look like him.

I do have some good times as a kid – it isn't all blood and guts, even though beatings always seem to follow, just as night follows day. But there are a few times when they don't – and one of them is when we go camping. I love being outdoors, out of the hellhole, and when we go camping most of the time we go with Dad's friends, and he'll never touch me when other people are around.

Today I'm going camping with my *good* dad – Funny Jock. I am eleven years old and we're going with one of the neighbours and his son – Big Geoff and Wee Geoff, who are a right pair of characters.

Big Geoff is actually fairly short for a man – around five foot three in height – but he's called Big Geoff because he weighs about sixteen stone and has quite a belly on him. He is hilarious, always laughing and joking and taking the piss out of Dad, which I love as he says things I've been dying to say for years.

Wee Geoff, on the other hand, is a skinny little lad, a few years younger than me, and nothing like his dad looks-wise – he has blond hair while Big Geoff has dark hair. But hanging around with Big Geoff for years has turned him into one of the funniest kids I've ever met. He'll stand fishing with his back to us and suddenly let out an almighty fart.

'Get oot and walk to the fart.'

Then Big Geoff will throw his bit in.

'That wisna a fart, that was an accident waitin' ti happen. You better check yir undies before yir cumin' in that tent later.'

I end up crying with laughter as they're like a double act.

We've arrived at a place called Crathy Bridge, not far from Aylyth at the foot of the Sidlaw Hills, which stretch from Perth to the north-east of Dundee, a distance of thirty miles. The bit we camp on is beside a river below the bridge. It's kind of in a field surrounded by trees with a six-foot embankment running down the side of a twenty-foot wide flowing river.

We always pitch a four-man tent a few metres back from the edge in case someone rolls out of the tent sleeping and has a midnight plunge, as the water is freezing. Everything is sorted and the adults are building a fire.

'Can we git the rods oot, Dad?' says Wee Geoff.

'Eh, but watch what yir dain' nixt ti that water,' Big Geoff replies. 'If yi fa' in there yi'll ken aboot it.'

'How, is it cald?'

'Dive in if yi want, and yi'll find oot.'

'I'll dae it if yi dae it,' says Wee Geoff.

Then Big Geoff, right on cue: 'Na yi winna yi fuckin' half-wit. Di yi want yir toby ti end up like a cocktail stick?'

'What, like yirs, Dad?'

He runs away from Big Geoff, laughing his head off.

'Awa yi go fishin' yi half-wit and stop nippin' mi hade.'

Wee Geoff and me are now standing about three feet from the edge, fishing away and watching the trout and salmon leaping out of the water, then reeling the line back in to try and drag it over the spot where the last fish splashed back in. I have my back to everyone as I'm watching a fish in the clear water trying to put the worm in front of its nose, then suddenly there's an almighty splash. I turn quickly as I think it's a massive salmon.

'Did you see the fish, Geoff?'

Then Dad dives in fully clothed. It still never registers until I see Wee Geoff's blond hair coming out of the water as Dad has got him back up. I reach my hand down to help the wee man, and there's an even bigger splash – this time I got soaked as well, and Dad and Wee Geoff nearly get crushed by

Big Geoff as he had noticed the wee man missing and has dived in to save him. He must have missed them by about an inch.

Everyone is soaked. Wee Geoff looks like a drowned rat, standing shivering by the fire with his eyes wide open from the temperature of the cold plunge pool he fell in.

After a while, once everyone's dry and OK, I have to go for a walk alone pretending to need the loo as these things are popping into my head while we're both being told off by them.

'What did eh tell yiz aboot going near the edge, yi eediots!'

I can see Wee Geoff trying not to laugh. But if I see someone trying to hold it in, it makes me worse and at this point I'm imagining the headlines in the paper the next day.

MAN SAVING BOY FROM DROWNING IS KILLED
BY BELLY FLOP FROM BOY'S FATHER!

I always try to see the funny side of situations to keep myself sane. Times like these are brilliant for me, as I can have my own personality and go exploring on my own in the fresh air. Away from the smell of drink and smoke and free from the thought of a hiding hanging over my head. The air is so pure that if you stand at the top of a hill and breathe in, you can feel your lungs getting rid of the city smoke and being replaced with clean air in seconds. And the wildlife and places to explore are out of this world.

I am a bit of an explorer as a kid. I'll walk for miles sometimes alone into the hills looking for any kind of wildlife or old run-down shacks. The places I find are magical. I'll be in the middle of the hills and stumble across old stone buildings with metal sheets on the roof.

Inside them people have left can openers or matches for anyone that's got lost in the hills. I have to sleep in one overnight once as the snow has turned into a blizzard, and there's no chance of going back down. I don't mind though as I'm on another adventure.

At least I have a few precious times like these as a kid. And I'm growing up now and seeing that there's more to life than the hellhole that I live in.

Chapter Eighteen

The Boy, the Dog and the Four-Foot Woman

For the last year Dad has been seeing a new woman – his second long-term girlfriend, Shelly, who has two children, one older than me called Claire and one younger called James.

I feel so sorry for Shelly. Dad goes for potential victims and that's Shelly all over. She's a very nice woman, a tiny little thing – probably only about seven and a half stone – with dark hair. I get on brilliantly with her, although of course she's never going to replace my mum who I'm spending more and more time with. Mum and I are becoming really close, even though I still never tell her what Dad's been doing to me.

As for Shelly, there's something a bit sheepish about her, like life has already kicked her about and got the better of her. Dad goes for that like he did with Mandy. The situation is similar – a single woman with two or three kids who's had a bit of a hard time when they were younger from shit husbands and he's got in there, he's coming to their rescue, the knight on the white charger, Mr Nice Guy …

And then he fucking gives them ten times worse than anything they've had in their life, ever.

He's very sneaky and cunning like that – he's psychotic but in a clever way, like when a hawk or eagle hovers above something and watches and watches, waiting to swoop down and devour its prey. He has those predatory instincts. He lulls them into a false sense of security and then attacks. It must have made him good on the football field too as he's a good tactician. But to get into someone's head and try and drive them crazy is just sick. I'm aged eleven and luckily have a strong head by now, but I can't imagine what it does to these women.

I have very little idea what her children Claire and James's attitude to him is as I can't ever take my eyes off him. I don't really ever look at anyone else. If he's in the room I focus all my attention on him. I have to. I just have to watch everything he's going to say and do next because I've been programmed to do that – and also because my survival depends on it. If I look away for a moment I'll get something in the side of my face.

They're really quiet, simple, normal kids, one has reddish hair, one black hair. They support Dundee United like I do and like everyone does. Claire never had a boyfriend at this time nor even when she was older. Maybe Dad's put her off men for life.

Claire and James sometimes cry when he's beating up Shelly but that doesn't mean much to me. My priority is to watch him, to be on my guard against him. And there's one consolation for me: while he's seeing Shelly and drinking more heavily I can sometimes be out playing football in the park. Instead of being stuck just with him as I was, I have more friends and can get away from the house. And for a while me and Bonnie can be out there playing and living a normal life.

Shelly lives in another tenement block at the end of St Nicholas Place, so it's not too far from the house we've moved to. I want to warn her what Dad's like as I've seen first hand what he did to his last long-term girlfriend Mandy, and also of course have distant memories about what he did to Mum, but I'm afraid that she might tell him, and I know only too well what will happen if she upsets him.

Shelly and Dad are always at our house rather than hers, as James and Claire might find it a bit weird having a new man in the house, whereas I'm just glad it isn't only me and him any more. I'm glad of the company.

Well, at first I'm glad. When Shelly is around, my beatings probably halve as Dad's now getting his fix by abusing us both – though fortunately Bonnie is a distant memory in his mind. She's safe, at least for the time being, except on the odd occasion when she pees in the kitchen if she hasn't been out all day and night when I'm at Mum's.

If Dad's beating up Shelly and I come in at ten o'clock at night she'll be sitting there with her lips burst and he's slouched on the chair saying, 'Hi son, where have yi been?'

I just look at him and I'm thinking, *You evil bastard*, but I can't say anything, so I just say, 'I've been at the park.'

'Go and get ready for bed.'

And then I hear him say, 'Yi shut yir fucking mouth,' to Shelly, as if I didn't know what he was doing.

I go upstairs, make sure Bonnie's all right – she'll be cowering under the bed and she'll crawl across the floor like a snake, really scared. Then I think, *Should I go back down, should I go back down?*

I leave it for a bit and then I'll say, 'I'm just going to get some toast,' and I slip downstairs in my pyjamas and walk past him.

'So where were yi?' he'll say again, as if he hadn't asked me already and I hadn't already answered him.

'I was at the park, Dad.'

Then he starts staring at me as I'm making toast.

'Fucking hurry up. Get to yir bed.'

And I think, right, get out of here quick, because he's now directing all his attention towards me. So I get my toast, go back upstairs and then I hear him beating her again.

Once or twice I've actually come down and opened the door again because Shelly's screaming, like he's going to kill

185

her. He puts his hands over her mouth to stop the screams and they go all muffled – '*Lmmggwww!*' – and I think he must be killing her and he just turns and punches me in the mouth and knocks me on the couch. Now he's smacking me and she's pleading with him, 'Jock, just leave him, leave him—' and then he boots her in the chin and she goes quiet for a bit.

If I manage to get to bed again I can still hear her sobbing or whimpering downstairs and I can't just lie there and listen to him battering her – I'd rather he was giving it to me than her.

Me and Shelly, we're both of us too weak and defenceless. She's too small to try and intervene when he's hitting me – she can't defend me any more than I can defend her.

What's weird, though, is that when she's in her own house she'll wait for her kids to get to bed, have a drink, and then come around to our house. It's almost like she comes over to get beaten up, because she knows he's been drinking. It's just stupid.

I think, *Why don't you run – get out of here!*

This thing he has over women is something I can't begin to understand. For someone to be such a psycho and for people not to pick up on it, or else to pick up on it but not do anything about it, is just plain bizarre and the older I get the more confused I am.

But these couple of years, between the ages of ten and twelve, are probably the most disturbing times of my already disturbed young life. As I approach my teenage years I'm becoming much more aware of what goes on in other kids' lives at home and I'm getting to realise that the nightmare that I'm living in is not the norm as I used to think it was.

Added to this, my frustration and rage at Dad's behaviour is building up and I'm getting more and more humiliated by having to sprint home from school when all my friends are free to stand around and socialise afterwards. At night I can never bring any of my friends home to sleep over. When I was younger I didn't know any better but now I feel that I have no life, that he's trying to crush the life out of me. Don't torture me, I often think, just finish me off.

Most of the time I just want to stop breathing after he beats me. I want him to kill me, hit me in the throat, choke me. One time I stand with a knife at my own wrists but I don't go through with it. I think, no I won't kill myself, I'll kill him. It's me or him, and it tips the balance in my mind over to killing him.

I don't know if you have ever lain in bed listening to a fully grown man interrogate and demolish a four-foot-tall woman. The only word I can ever come up with is sick! I actually look forward to him beating me as what he's doing to her makes me feel worse than if I'd been the victim. I'd rather take a beating than listen to her scream and plead.

Some nights I whisper to her, 'Stop talking, Shelly, that's what he enjoys.'

In the mornings Shelly sits in the living room with black eyes and bruised arms.

'Do yi want a cup of tea and some toast, Charlie?'

'No thanks, Shelly.' I'm dying to tell her to run while I distract him.

'He's quite capable of making his own breakfast.'

You heartless bastard, you're not even sorry. I'm gonna fuckin' kill you one day.

I'm glad he isn't a mind reader.

I stand in the kitchen listening to her apologising for nothing. I'm actually physically sick one morning, when I see what he's just done to her. The white bits of her eyes are totally red and it reminds me of a horror film I saw on telly. Pictures are now popping into my head of what it must have been like for Mum, the pain she must have gone through. I really want to kill him now. There's no two ways about it – he has to die.

I nearly do it once. I nearly kill him. That's about a month and a half after I change my mind about killing myself and decide to kill him instead.

It's a few weeks after my twelfth birthday and he's left me in a horrible mess one night and fallen asleep on the floor. I can hear him snoring from my bedroom so I walk downstairs into the kitchen and take a ten-inch knife from the drawer.

My body is shaking with fear and the adrenaline is making me whisper things to myself.

'Put it in the middle, it'll go right through.' As he's on his side with his back to me, I'm trying to calculate if the blade is long enough to go through his back, and burst his heart.

I promise you now, with my hand on my heart, if he had been facing towards me that night he would be dead. That's the only thing that saved him.

But after this night, after I don't kill him, I get more angry and more frustrated with myself for not having gone through with it. What kind of a wimp am I?

As the months roll on, Dad and Shelly split up, get back together, split up again, and on and on it goes. I can never understand why she keeps coming back for more; it's like he has some weird control over other people as he does me. Sober he's funny, generous, always laughing, and has a lot of friends, but everyone must know what he is doing, and what he's like with a drink. At least, that's what I keep telling myself. So why does nobody blank him or get him done, report him, anything? Why doesn't anyone see what he's done to me – and now to Shelly?

As a twelve year old I've got little experience of what goes on anywhere else. I've never been out of Dundee apart from our trips to Glenshee and I know nothing about social workers. I've never heard of the term 'child abuse'. I only know the hell, horror and sickness that are my normal daily life with him. But I do know how devious and clever Dad can be in explaining away any signs of the beatings he deals out to me and Shelly.

And I know how Shelly and I collude with each other by denying that anything's wrong, and hiding ourselves away until the bruises fade. Dad's friends and the community around us also take part in this big deception by turning a blind eye to what's going on, ignoring it or simply regarding it as none of their business. If people in Dundee have 'domestics', that's their own private affair and it's not for outsiders to interfere in what goes on behind closed doors.

Of course I'm only too aware now of the catastrophic role drink plays – how it turns Dad, sometimes in an instant, from Dr Jekyll into Mr Hyde – and I'm beginning to realise a few other things too. Although I can never understand why or how you can treat a kid with the same regard a butcher treats a dead carcass, I have started to gather, from a remark or two dropped by Mum, just how badly Dad was treated by his father. But I still think he was lucky to be kicked out of home at the age of twelve. I pray for a quick death or that the house will burn down with both of us in it.

I keep thinking he's driving Shelly to have a breakdown – '*Just kill me!*' I hear her screaming some nights. But she keeps coming back for more, until finally one night he gives her such a battering that even she's had enough.

After that night she never comes back.

Later on, when Shelly and her kids are out of his life, I feel too embarrassed to go near them just as I did with Mandy and her family. We're like fellow hostages or prisoners of war who share the same shameful secrets of our captivity, and the best thing I can do is to keep away from them and let it be. I don't want my face to remind them of anything that he's done.

But I wish I could do what Shelly's done and simply walk away. To be out of that torture den would be heaven to me.

Chapter Nineteen

Scared to Laugh

I'm now twelve and for the last year, since I was eleven, I've been going to secondary school – Lawside Academy. Although it's called 'academy' it's just a normal school.

At primary school my report cards were terrible. The best of them would say things like, 'Could do better if he wasn't trying to make a joke out of it.' I'd bounce a rubber off the back of a teacher's head or if somebody made a fart noise I'd be on the floor. Instead of not moving a muscle in case Dad hit me, the battleground in school was a matter of not moving in case I giggled.

While I'm still at primary school I go on a three-day visit to Lawside for a trial period and I nearly get suspended during this visit. We're in a big group and we're getting shown around the school – 'This is Mr So and So, who'll be your English teacher, and this is Mrs Such and Such, who'll be your Maths teacher' – and I'm getting bored and fed up with it so I decide to wander off and look for my friend Paul – Mandy's son – while they're still in the middle of all the 'this is so and so'-ing.

I open a classroom door and the teacher's standing there teaching a class and I say, being cheeky, 'Sorry Miss, do you know Paul Campbell?'

'Are you on the three-day visit?' she says. 'Quick, you'd better get back to your group.'

'Oh shut up, you half-wit,' I say, and walk out of the classroom.

When they take me to see the Head, he says, 'We could make sure you do not come near this school,' and then lectures me for an hour on how I'll have to buck my ideas up.

But they do let me go to Lawside and I enjoy my first year there. I get to meet a lot of people from different areas of Dundee. There are already gangs – people from different primary schools all coming to secondary school, Catholics and Protestants.

When I get on with a teacher and I'm interested I give it a hundred per cent – as I do for Maths, English, PE and Art. When I'm in art class I'm just left alone to draw or paint, which I love. If someone says do a still life from these objects, or do a drawing from this photo of a Charles Renie Mackintosh chair – I'll do it and get lost in it. I love drawing and if something interests me then it's great. The teacher will just pop over every now and again and say, 'That's good.'

I love it when I'm left alone with nobody to bug me, especially if I'm encouraged, like in PE when I'm in the middle of a field or bouncing around on a trampoline. I'm using my energy, really enjoying it. I also love English and Maths.

As it has been earlier on in my life, school is a blessed relief, an oasis of freedom for me. I've met loads of new mates, and Paul – the eldest son of Dad's first girlfriend Mandy, who is a year above me – has once again taken me under his wing and looks after me at school. He's always been like a big brother to me, even though I now also have Tommy and Bobby, my real brothers.

By this time Paul has blanked out a lot of what went on with Dad and Mandy when we all lived together. He knew it happened, as he was dragged down to watch his mother getting drowned in the bath, but I think he chooses to forget, and I can't blame him. I wish I could forget, but I'm with Dad night and day, and I can only blank so much out of the hours of punishment I receive daily.

The people in my year are all cut from the same cloth – well, my classes anyway. They are all mental, but in a good way. In six out of my ten subjects my desk ends up outside the door. In my primary school I learnt how to use comedy to cover up how I really felt and to get by, and because I've always loved a good joke, and now I've become a master at it. If someone does something and the whole class is sniggering I often find myself laughing more at them trying to hold their laughs in. It's like when you're in church and you're not supposed to giggle. Or that scene in *Monty Python's Life of Brian*.

There are two or three guards and Pontius Pilate who has a lisp (the character played by Michael Palin can't say his Rs) is about two inches from their faces shouting about some bloke called Biggus Dickus and his wife Incontinentia Buttocks – and the guards mustn't laugh. My classmates are like those guards, the sides of their mouths twitching, shoulders shaking from the inside, trying not to laugh and making these little muffled mouse squeaks.

When I watch that film I can't control myself any more than I can in class. It's the thought of not being allowed to do something that sets me off. In a very weird way, it's like not being allowed to move a muscle on the couch in case Dad beats me. Except it's the opposite: instead of the pain of not being allowed to cry, not being allowed to laugh only makes me want to laugh more.

I do well in some subjects – normally if the teacher has a sense of humour. If he or she is a misery arse then that means a fail for me.

My favourite teachers are Mr White, the geography teacher, and Mrs Macdonald, who teaches English. I like them for totally different reasons; Mr White is an out and out nutter but a very intelligent man who knows people better than they know themselves, whereas Mrs Macdonald is helpful and very patient with people who don't pick things up as quickly as others.

I'm in Mr White's class one day, sitting at the back talking to Calum (yeah, Calum Patterson is in my year and class again – I can't get rid of him).

'Have you seen wa United have signed?' says Calum.

'No, wha is it?' I ask.

'*Right boys*! Stand up.' He has caught us talking.

'Sorry, sir, I was just—'

'No, no, Charlie don't tell me, you and Calum stand up and tell the class.'

Calum loves it. He springs up out of his chair. 'Come on partner.'

Oh oh! Calum normally comes out with some wisecrack and I'll start laughing my head off, then it will be the old desk outside treatment.

'OK lads, fire away,' says Mr White.

'I'll take this one, Charlie. Right class, cheers for coming along the day.'

'Get on with it, smart arse.'

'Dinna rush me sir, this is important info.'

I'm starting to snigger, as just looking at his mad face is enough to get me going anyway.

'What were you talking about then, Calum?'

'Well, sir, Charlie wiz asking me if I died and could come back as sumin', what wid it be?'

I look at him in amazement. 'What are you goin' on aboot?'

'No, Charlie, I have to tell them.' The whole class is engrossed in this utter crap story that he's making up as he goes along.

'That's no what we're sayin, sir,' I protest.

'No, Charlie, let him finish, I'm on the edge of my seat here.'

'As I was saying folks,' Calum spins back around towards the class, 'I was telling me amigo Charlieo that there is two things I canna choose between.'

'Come on, get on with it.'

I can't believe Mr White is letting this farce continue.

'Number One, I would like to come back as a cat, because they come and go as they please, lay about all day and don't listen to a thing anyone says.'

'And Number Two, and hurrying it up,' Mr White prompts. The class are starting to laugh, staring at us both standing there like the Two Ronnies. I don't think anyone's prepared for what Calum says next.

'Number Two, sir. I want to come back as a woman's bike seat!'

The class collapses in laughter.

I look straight at Mr White trying not to laugh. 'He's full o' crap, sir!'

'Right go 'n site doon the two o' yis!' He has a massive smirk on his face as he knows it's just Calum being his usual crazy self. If it had been any other teacher Calum's feet wouldn't have touched the floor.

The Nipper

Mrs Macdonald's class is the complete opposite. She's calm and helpful. You can ask her anything at any time in class if you're stuck with something. She's in her early thirties, blonde bobbed hair, a real stunner, and she looks a bit like Michelle Pfeiffer. I think she's my first love.

In her classroom the desks have chairs on both sides, so some people have their backs to her and some are facing her. Calum sits directly across the desk from me. He will ask me to shout her over and ask her a question, as when she's talking to you, she'll lean over your shoulder to look close at your work. She sometimes wears a white blouse with the top two buttons undone in the summer when it's hot. Calum's a fly man, he has a peek down her top as she leans over my shoulder. He's off his rocker, but I'm sure she plays up to it – at least she seems to fall for it every time which makes me think she's doing it deliberately and that she's loving it really.

High school is a great escape for me as no matter what's going on at home I always have friends and teachers I can have a laugh with and so blank out all the badness in my life. Through school I am meeting more and more kids from different areas and backgrounds, and most of them have a story to tell. Some are picked on by other family members, some of their dads or mums are in jail, some have eating disorders and one has been sexually abused by their uncle. When I was younger we didn't talk about these things, but now we're verging on teenagers, we're prepared to be more open about what goes on at home.

I am a little relieved that other people are in the same boat as me, as when I was younger I always thought I deserved it and it was my fault that Mum left, then Mandy. But looking at the people I'm now friends with, I know it's Dad that is sick and twisted and it's his fault. These kids are good people, just looking for a bit of normality away from the torture dens we have become accustomed to.

Chapter Twenty

Water Fight

As I move into my teenage years, I'm starting to develop a split personality just like Dad. Most of the time at school, for instance, I'm cheerful and put on a happy front. I love jokes and clowning around and making other kids laugh.

But there's this other side to me: an explosive anger which has been brewing for years and it's starting to erupt on odd occasions. My life seems to be more up and down than a fiddler's elbow, with joy one minute and misery the next.

Back in school, I have been kicked out of yet another class, with my desk in the corridor. It's the French class. Teaching you a lot of crap about '*La pomme est sur la table*'. If you went on holiday to France and said that to someone they'd call the nearest mental hospital and have you picked up within minutes.

I hate it when people talk down to me but the nicer someone is to me the more they'll get out of me.

So I'm in the corridor with my head on the desk, trying to have a kip as it's a double period. I've been kicked out for saying 'Haw, hee, haw' in a French accent. It's something Big Geoff likes to say if a foreign girl walks past when we're on a campsite. I don't know what it means but Mr Henry never liked me from day one, so it's probably nothing.

I'm out cold, fast asleep at my desk in the corridor, when I feel a thud on the back of my head and suddenly I'm soaked with water. I jump out of the chair and clock out of the corner of my eye the ladies' toilet door slowly closing.

I let out a loud yelp when the water hits me, as it's freezing. Instantly the classroom door opens.

'What are you doing, boy? What is this noise for?'

'Someone's hit me with a water bomb, sir.'

'Do not distract my class again, there is no one here.'

This loony thinks I've soaked myself with water to get his attention and make the class laugh at me.

'But sir, I—'

'No buts! Just keep quiet.'

I hate people stopping me mid-sentence, but I can't say anything, as I would be off to the Head's office, Mr Gleeson. He's a big tall man about six foot four, with a great purple whisky nose and a reputation for excluding or expelling people who disrupt his school. So I decide to bite my tongue.

But when Frenchy goes back in and closes the door I hear someone laughing in the girls' toilet so I head into the boys' loo and fill a metal paper-towel holder with water, then wait outside the ladies.

Two heads pop out and look right up the corridor to where I was sitting earlier. Unfortunately for them I'm to the left of the door.

Splash! Straight over both their heads. It's Natalie and Kelly, a couple of girls who come from Kirkton, about ten minutes from St Mary's. They're a right pair of nutters, always up for a laugh, but the joke's on them this time. I cover their pretty little red heads and then run back to my desk, put my head down and pretend I haven't moved. The screams they make when I soak them cause three different teachers to come out of their classrooms to find out what's going on.

'What the hell was that noise, Charlie?'

'Two girls ran out of that door, sir, chasing each other.'

'Idiots!'

'I know, sir, some people are just mad.'

'Get back to your work.'

Then he shuts the door and the other teachers follow suit. The girls have gone off somewhere – they should be in class but they're dodging teachers and skipping lessons.

I put my head down and doze off again, as I've hardly had any sleep at home with all the shit that's going on. The next thing I know I'm inside a boxlike object and am soaked from head to foot – and I mean everywhere. It's pitch black.

I stand up real quick and pull this wastepaper bin off my head.

The girls have gone and filled this massive plastic bin with water to the top and dragged it up to my desk. I don't have a clue how they managed to get it up above my head as it's huge. Then they've planted it over me and run off down the corridor. I'm now standing there like a drowned rat, and seriously pissed off because I've been woken up a second time.

The door of the classroom flies open.

'*What are you doing now?*'

Well, that's it. I explode.

'*Do you think I'd put a bin o' water over mi ane hade. Yi fuckin' idiot?*'

Frenchy's mouth opens and his jaw drops.

'What did you just say?'

'ARE YOU DEAF AS WELL AS FUCKIN' THICK?'

'Right boy, Mr Gleeson's office.'

'*I don't give a shit*,' I say, walking down the corridor to Gleeson's office.

'Sit there.'

'*Shut up, you gimp*,' I reply.

He knocks on the door and then goes into Gleeson's office. While I'm waiting outside I've started to calm down and am now thinking of Dad and what he might do if I get suspended or, worse, expelled.

Frenchy comes back out and walks back towards his class, while I sit outside waiting for the shit to hit the fan. Through the glass in the double doors from another corridor I see Natalie and Kelly being marched towards me by another teacher who has seen the girls running out of the corridor and stopped them to ask why they aren't in class, then seen me soaking wet with the bin they launched over my head. He's then put two and two together.

They come and sit beside me, laughing at the fact that I look like I've slipped in the swimming pool with all my clothes on.

'Please don't tell it was us.'

'Dinna be daft. I never seen yiz anyway.'

'I'm gonna get killed when I get home,' Natalie butts in.

'Not as bad as what I'm gonna get. Just tell them you were running because you needed a pee! It's worth a go.'

Then the second teacher goes into Gleeson's office and puts in his tuppence about the girls and comes back out.

'I don't know what you're laughing at. He's not in a good mood.'

'I'm not laughing, sir, I'm nervous!' Natalie says. She's crapping herself but she uses the old laugh-and-it-might-go-away technique, like me.

Suddenly the door opens. Gleeson is standing there in his pinstriped suit, staring over his glasses that are perched on his big purple nose.

'Charlie, you first.'

I stand up and walk in, closing the door behind me.

'What's happening with you, boy?' His voice is very calm as he leans back in his chair.

'Nothing, sir—'

'Sit down.' He points at a seat at the other side of his desk. 'Sorry, carry on.'

'I was outside Frenchy's classroom—'

'Let me stop you there – his name is *not* Frenchy.'

'Sorry sir, I was outside Mr Henry's classroom doing my work and someone put a bin full of water over my head.'

'Was it the girls outside?'

'I don't know, sir, I never seen anyone as my head was in the bin.'

'So you are telling me you never heard or saw anyone sneak up on you – two people with a massive bin.'

'I was sleeping, sir.'

'You don't come to school to sleep, you come to learn.'

'I know, sir, please dinna suspend me, my life winna be worth living if you do.'

'What about the abusive language you directed at Mr Henry. No one in this school can talk to teachers like that.'

'I know, sir, but he had already kicked me out the class for making one comment and then accused me of putting a bin of water on my own head. Are you gonna tell mi dad and suspend me sir?'

'No Charlie, I'm not, but I can't let you walk around in those clothes and catch a cold.'

'Thanks sir, thanks a lot.'

'Don't thank me yet, son. I'll be back in a second, wait there.'

He walks out of the office, leaving me confused as to what he meant, but it's not long before I find out. Two minutes later he comes back into the office and hands me a box.

'Put these on and leave your wet clothes over the chair,' he says and goes out again.

What a good man, he's given me clean clothes! Then I open the box and pull out some of the most old-fashioned, oversized clothes you could imagine.

There are brown flares with a 36-inch waist; a white and yellow flower patterned shirt with collars that nearly touch my waist; a pink and purple Paisley kipper tie four inches wide; and a pair of size-nine platform shoes. I have to tie the trousers with another school tie so they'll stay up.

Fair play, he would rather humiliate me than get me done in, I respect him for that. Even so, I look like a total plonker.

It's right on the lunch bell as I put on my last item, and my hair is slapped over my forehead like George McFly from *Back to the Future*.

Mr Gleeson comes back in and tells me I can pick my clothes up later and to keep my temper under control. I think he means my language.

'Thanks again, sir!'

'Stay out of trouble.' I can tell he's dying to laugh. 'Go on, have some lunch.'

I walk out the office past Natalie and Kelly and not surprisingly they break down in fits of laughter.

'What have they done to you?' Kelly is slapping the bench. Tears are running down her face.

The small square outside the Head's office is getting busy with people going into the dinner hall. I wait until the lunch hall is packed and then pick my moment. Gleeson may have thought he would embarrass me into behaving, but what he doesn't know is that this is an excellent opportunity for me to be the centre of attention.

I stroll into that dinner hall with a bounce and a swagger in my step – just like John Travolta as he walks along the street in the opening scene of *Saturday Night Fever.*

'Alright ladies?' I say as I walk past a couple of the older girls.

The whole dinner hall is laughing – there's even some wolf whistling and shouts of 'Wayhey!' Other people look on in bemusement, as if they thought I actually dressed like that.

It's hilarious. I'm just glad no one has a camera.

I'm now into my teens and starting to go through puberty. I've met loads of new friends from school that I hang around with at night – but I'm only allowed to do so by Dad under very strict conditions.

At home it's getting more like being in the army than living with a parent. Dad seems to have turned into a sergeant major overnight. School finishes at 3.45 p.m. and I have to be home by 4 p.m. or 1600 hours on the dot, or before.

There's usually a period between when I get home at four and when I have tea at 6.30 p.m. when he isn't drinking. It's like a respite period for me, except that I'm always waiting for the drinking to start up, so I can never relax. If I've done something wrong and he's still sober, he'll have a verbal go at me and then say, 'I'm going to the VG for eggs.' The VG is the local food store.

I think, *Here it comes*, and try and get as much food in me as I can, because I know what will happen when he gets back. Sure enough, he's bought the vodka and soon the beatings start.

And now even if I'm just one minute late after four, once he starts drinking that is all the trigger he needs to unleash frenzied attacks on me for hours and send me to bed at twelve o'clock starving. But if I manage to make it home before 4 p.m. he'll allow me to go out again after supper and stay out until nine o'clock, but with the same rules as before.

That's out of the question this evening, though. It's 4.04 p.m. on Tuesday, 11 July 1989. I've arrived home from school four minutes late and Dad is waiting for me.

Chapter Twenty-One

Four Minutes Past Four

*H*e's sober but he's got that look in his eyes – wary, watchful, the lids turned down at the corners, the finger pointing. He could be on the warpath but I'm not quite sure.

'What have I told yi about being late? I worry if you're no in at the right time.'

'Sorry, Dad, I wiz talking to Calum.'

'Is that it, yi wir talking to Calum?'

'I just lost track o' time, Dad.'

'I'm goin' to the shops fir stuff fir tea, go and get cheenged.'

'OK.'

He leaves the house and I head upstairs to get changed. I'm relieved and not really worried as he seems quite calm compared to normal, even though he's just split up with Shelly again. He normally flips after Shelly leaves, as I think he enjoys hitting her more than me.

He comes back with his usual VG bag with stuff for tea and his voddy and Coke. He used to just drink a bottle every night but he's now getting through a whole litre every night. It beats me where he gets the money to fund his drinking habit. I suppose he's still crawling around the roofs drunk. I'm sitting watching TV after doing some dishes and folding clothes up that have dried on the clothes horse thing. While tea is on he's getting stuck into the voddy drinking.

It's very quick – he's drinking down one glass after another. Maybe it's an excuse for what's about to happen.

He's finished in the kitchen and brings two plates through, one each, and I get some forks and knives and salt and sauce.

'There's fucking dog hairs awar, fucking mutt.'

'I'll hoover up after tea, Dad.'

'Yi could have done it when eh wiz in the shops, but it's arite, yi're gonna dae it after tea.'

He's starting to get very sarcastic, always a bad sign, but he still doesn't have an excuse to start anything.

Then I look down on my plate and think, shit! There's a plum tomato slap bang on top of my egg and chips – the juice is all over it. He knows that every time I've tried to eat a tomato in my life, I've heaved and puked. He even tried to force-feed me one a couple of years ago, and I took a beating rather than eat it, as I'm allergic to them and can't stomach them.

210

I pick a couple of chips from around the side, the ones with no juice on them, trying to act normal, but he's seen me eating around it and places his fork and knife down on his plate.

'What's up, Charlie?' He looks pissed off.

'Nothing.'

'What the fuck's up now?'

'I can't eat tomatoes, Dad, I'll puke mi ringer.'

He stands up and walks towards me. 'Geeze yir plate then,' he says, putting his hand out.

I pass the plate to him. 'Thanks, Dad.'

'No problem, I'll just cook yir tea, don't eat it, I'm loaded wi money.'

More sarcasm! Great! He's still standing beside me with the plate in his hand. Then he says, 'Come in the kitchen and pick something else.'

I stand up and walk towards him as he turns his back on me to go into the kitchen. I normally kept an eye on him when he's drinking just in case he flips as most of the time his personality will change in an instant, but on this occasion he's a bit annoyed but doesn't seem too aggressive.

I look down to avoid standing on the remote control that's on the floor. And as I look back up, the plate I've handed him comes crashing into my face, all over the wall and onto the dog-hair-covered floor. The tomato in my face is the worst thing, though, as I hate them as much as I hate him.

'Yi will fuckin' eat every last bit o' that dinner.'

211

I don't know if the plate has cut me or it's the tomato juice all over my top, but I'm panicking like mad. And he's at that drunk stage when he's still quite strong but totally mental. He grabs the back of my hair and pushes my face towards the wall.

'Eat it, yi ungrateful bastard. Lick the fuckin' wa, clean it, eat it!' he shouts.

'Dad, please, I can't!' The thought of going near that tomato is making me heave.

Smash into the wall with my face again, one hand on my hair and the other on the back of my neck.

'FUCKING EAT IT!'

I started licking all this slop off the wall.

'Get the whole lot, yi cunt!'

I am ready to blow chunks.

'Dad, please, I've had enough! I'm gonna puke!'

'Oh look, yir food's on my carpet. Get down there, yi bastard.'

Dragging me down to the floor by the hair.

'Dad stop it, I'm gonna spew.'

Grabbing crushed up tomato and egg and ramming it into my face, holding my nose so I'll open my mouth. The tomato's covered in Bonnie's hair.

'Chew it, yi cunt, go on swallow, that's it, chew it, tomatoes are good for yi.'

'Dad, please!' I say, choking and puking on the carpet and onto his hand.

'Maybe if yi hoovered, then yi wouldna be chewing on dog hair now would yi.' He notices the sick on his hand. 'Yi dirty little cunt, yi puke on my carpet, now yi eat it.'

'Please stop, Dad!'

'What's up? Do yi no like eggs?'

'*Arrggg, what are yi dain this fir?*' I scream at the top of my lungs.

'Oh are yi gitin' a bit o' a temper now yir gitin alder. Go on then, I'll give yi a free shot. Go on tough guy.'

He has taken one step back and put his chin out towards me. I just stare at him and never say anything.

'Go on then, yi ken yi want ti. Come on, BIG MAN! Have yi found a few hairs on yir balls? Come on, hit me! I'll tell yi one thing, yi'll have to kill me.'

He walks towards me with his arms by his side, fists clenched as I walk backwards towards the living-room door. He kicks the door closed as I try to escape, so I'm now stuck in the corner, trapped like a lightweight being mauled by a heavyweight.

The punches are coming from all angles; kicks and knees are then added, and a few toe punts in the balls nearly finish me off. He just keeps hitting and stamping as I slide down the door, blood splattered all over the white gloss door and cream curtains.

It's the longest hiding I've ever had; it goes on and on and on, getting more painful as areas are hit for the seventh and eighth time. As if that isn't bad enough, he's poking my eyes, nipping the backs of my legs with his massive hands and biting my hands, so I'd stop trying to block the punches. The weirdo is even actually trying to stamp my balls into oblivion. I think subconsciously he is hoping to stop another generation of people that might turn out like him.

Through the long night that follows I try a few times to escape but he's slowed his drinking down to prove he's still the boss. I think he's clicked onto the fact that I will bob and weave out of the way when he's really pissed.

My anger the next day is uncontrollable. I'm off school again with a note but when I meet up with my pals the next evening, I go on a one-man self-destruct mission.

All my friends that I hang around with at the time have seen the mess my face is in, but I don't care, I'm not gonna hide it any more. I have to get some of this anger that had built up inside out, and I don't care who or what I release it on.

I go out that night wrecking things, smashing windows, kicking cats, putting gas bottles in sheds and blowing them up, anything that I can destroy.

Chapter Twenty-Two

The Rogues

That will be the last really bad beating Dad ever gives me. It's certainly not the last time he beats me – he gives me loads more – but it's the last serious one as I'm getting bigger and stronger between the ages of fourteen and fifteen.

For one thing, I've started going to kick-boxing classes. Something has switched in me. I've finally decided that I won't be a punch bag ever again. If anyone's going to do the punching, it will be me. I've come more under the influence of my big brother Tommy, too, who already at the age of fifteen has became a Scottish amateur boxing champion.

And I've started up a gang in St Mary's with Calum. We call it The Rogues. It's halfway between a club and a gang and you have to do loads of mad stuff to prove yourself and become a member. I've lost it at this point. All those years of built-up frustration, pain and suppressed anger have just

215

burst out of me. I'm thinking *fuck my dad, fuck the world and fuck anyone who crosses my path*.

Dad has succeeded. He's turned me into a monster like him – only I would never pick on women or kids. I start on people's property and later go on to fully grown men. The Rogues Club I start when I am fourteen involves a lot of different things. We're a group of angry, alienated kids with bad attitudes – years later we'd have been called Asbo kids – looking for things to vent our anger on and destroy.

We start by wrecking cars and blowing sheds up with the gas bottles stored in them. Then smashing windows on a points system: the further away you are, or the bigger and stronger the item, the more points you get.

We have around twelve members from the St Mary's area, with a name chart, with all of our names on it. That's to keep a record of who's the biggest rogue – who's caused the most destruction basically. And as usual I'm at the top of the leader board.

One of the lads who's close behind me puts a garden gate through someone's front window and ends up on the front page of the *Telegraph* newspaper. Not to be outdone, as I hate getting beaten, I fill a container full of dog dirt and smash it through someone's window. I know it's disgusting, but the more beatings I get from Dad, the more angry I become and the more determined to heap misery on the rest of the world.

We make up descriptive slogans for everything we do. For instance, one of the other lads calls my dog-dirt grenade 'A

Rather Large Stink Bomb'. Soon The Rogues start to get bigger with more and more people joining, so that more activities are added, like bouncing cars into the middle of the road and setting fire to things.

Then there's bogus milk money collecting. As none of us has a penny we watch people doing a milk round in the morning and follow them, writing down the numbers of the doors that have a delivery. Then on a Friday, we go half an hour earlier than the real milk boy and collect his money with a bogus book. I'm getting worse and worse with each new scam I dream up, as I now realise that most of the kids I hang around with have smart clothes on. And as Dad never has money to buy me things, stealing is now my mission.

I'll go into the local shop and get one of the lads to distract the shopkeeper, while I steal the milk tokens from behind the counter. These are worthless to most people, but I have a friend working for a dairy firm that thinks they're gold dust, as he can cash them in. I'll swap him the tokens for his old Pringle jumpers. And hey presto, I'm one of the lads without anyone knowing any better. Then I'll come home from school some nights, and Dad will be sitting wearing them, covered in soot from sweeping chimneys. At times like this I walk along to the shops, kicking fences and punching cars in a rage, as I'm back to my old scruffy self again. I'm thinking of how I can get even with him and of the next scam to kit myself out.

The older lads are gang fighting with the Dales and Kirton at the time, and I really want a piece of it. I want to hit somebody, and not worry about being killed or kicked out, or whether I'll be homeless or out in a home. The Rogue thing isn't fuelling my anger – in the end it's more of a laugh to me. But now I don't want to laugh. I want to destroy. So I walk down towards the Dales past St Leonard's Church.

The Dales are another gang – or scheme, as we call them – not far from St Mary's. Both gangs will meet in the middle of a football pitch, while the girls sit on a massive stone teapot in the park to get a good view of the action. It really annoys me most of the time, as it's a bit like cat and mouse at first – you chase us then we chase you. There are only a couple of people standing in the middle that are prepared to have a punch up.

I love it when nobody runs. We collide in the middle like a scene from *Braveheart* and every person running towards me looks like Evil Jock. Well, in my head they do. It's mostly just hands and feet that are used, but there's one bloke you have to watch out for. If you have someone on the ground giving them a hiding you always have to watch your back.

This bloke is nicknamed 'Animal'. He's about four foot high, really skinny with dark hair and a boxer's face, like most of the kids have, as they're all getting battered at home like I am. He'll glide around the mass brawl looking for targets. His calling card is to stick a knife in people's arse cheeks. If you hear a scream you know exactly where Animal is.

Later on I hear that he's been killed in a knife attack. What goes around comes around I guess.

The fights are giving me a buzz and I don't care if Dad batters me when I get home as I'm now finally learning to duck and dive his punches and kicks. I'm still not old enough or brave enough – or maybe stupid and reckless enough – to dare to lash out at him, as I'm still too frightened of him, but I'm getting much better at defending myself. You might call this long overdue, but I'm making him miss and he's getting tired a lot quicker than normal. Plus, of course, we're both getting older and time's now definitely on my side, no problem. I used to just lie there and take the hours of torture, but now I'm getting quicker, and wiser to when he will attack.

The times I spend rolling around with people my own age are now getting more and more frequent. And weapons are being added. We will all break brush handles and wooden fences down to arm ourselves, then walk down to the football pitch like a mini drunken army, marching close together.

'Y-M-B, who are we? We are the boys who rule Dundee.' At the top of our lungs, so the other gang can hear us coming.

One night we're running up the middle of the pitch, towards the Dales gang, when I see this silver thing flying through the air at the last minute, coming towards my face. There's no time to get out of the way as it smashes me in the forehead.

219

I fall backwards onto the grass and can hear a hissing noise. I think for a moment it's my brain making the noise, until I look beside me and see a can of Tennant's lager with a pin-hole in it.

Yep, you guessed it. I've been hit with a full can of beer and yet again I have another egg sticking out of my forehead. But things like that don't bother me now, as it's a battle scar to prove you never ran. As long as it never hits the back of your head, you're fine.

I sometimes take Bonnie to the gang fights with me. Even though Dad gets away with beating me, Bonnie never lets anyone else get away with it. There are never that many people hanging around if I have Bonnie with me. She'll stand in front of me and show her teeth – not growling, just lifting her top lip to unveil her huge wolflike nashers.

A few of the lads say they're thinking of joining the Cadets and ask me what I think. I'm up for anything by this stage – life is starting to get more interesting and exciting. Only a couple of years ago, I just wanted it all to end. When I saw the bodies of people who had thrown themselves off the multi-storey tenements I wanted to be one of them. But now I don't want to die any more, as my fear has turned into hate and anger.

So we join the Blackwatch Cadets in St Mary's. We've got army uniforms and we're ready to fight for the country. Well, until they wake you up at five in the morning to go on a ten-mile jog. I'm up for the war side of it, but I don't join it to run after people. I thought that was what a gun was for, so you didn't have to chase people.

I'm enjoying this period of my life, but Dad is drinking a lot more heavily and any money he has now seems to go on drink. I don't need him any more though. I have petty crime to pay for my army uniform and boots, and I'm doing a paper round to save to go to England. It's a two-week holiday with the Cadets to a place near Southport called Altcar which has a rifle range. Cadets from everywhere go there once a year to learn how to fire real guns, go sniping through the grass and go on five-mile runs at stupid o'clock in the morning.

In the end before I go I have to call Mum to borrow some money as Dad's found my stash, and spent it all on drink. I am in a quiet, controlled rage about this but it's so much of a habit for me to keep my feelings about Dad bottled up that as usual I say nothing about it to Mum. I don't need to tell her anyway, as she's probably guessed already. It's just one more thing that I log in the back of my brain for the day of reckoning. Besides, at this point I just want Dad to die, so I don't want to tell anyone anything about me and him, especially Mum, as I don't want to incriminate her or involve her in what I'm planning to do to him.

Mum's always good with money and gifts. I love having Christmas presents from her – it's always designer trainers and tops or something that you can never afford yourself. She isn't loaded though, it's through a catalogue. Dad buys me things as well, but they're normally accompanied by a black eye or burst nose a couple of hours later, if anything is marked or has a slight scrape. I think he's forgotten that I'm a teenage lad, the way he goes on.

'What the fuck is that on yir trainer?'

Grass, you wanker! You should go outside more if you've forgotten what it looks like.

When I get back from Altcar I'm told to hand my kit back and I'm never allowed to go again. They've kicked me out of the Cadets. When I went there and joined no one told me some arsehole a couple of years older would decide to scream in my face from around an inch away while spitting all over me. What did he expect me to do, kiss him?

I did give him a kiss – it was of the Glasgow variety.

On my return I decide to look for something else to keep me occupied. Bonnie had got out one night alone and ended up pregnant to some other dog. So I can't really take her up to Clatto or near anyone as she's getting a bit temperamental. So I join back up with The Rogues again.

This time around we do things that are a little more weird and stupid, bordering on dangerous, like Shitealight! You pick up loads of dog dirt in a newspaper, put it on someone's doorstep, set the paper on fire, and then knock on the door and hide behind the hedge watching through the gaps to see the outcome. People open the door, see the fire and try to stamp it out, covering their slippers in dog shit.

Another one is tying two doors together. In the Closies, the tenement blocks, the doors are opposite each other. We'll get some washing line or rope and make it about five inches longer than door-to-door, then we'll tie the ends to the handles and knock on both doors. After that we stand there and hurl insults at the people as they pull the rope back and forward, screaming that we're dead when they get out.

I'll be standing there in fits of laughter as Calum Patterson's favourite trick is to push his privates between his legs to make him look like a women. Then he'll turn his back to the door, bend over, and talk in a woman's voice.

'Has anyone seen my washing rope?'

I'm on the floor, as the men behind the doors are foaming at the mouth with anger, pulling each other's doors back and forward.

'You're a dead man, dirty little bastard!' Then the two house-owners will start getting frustrated with each other.

'Stop pulling the fucking door, yi half-wit, I'm pulling mine.'

'Wha are you calling a half-wit!'

We then take the rope off as both doors close, and walk downstairs as if we had left them tied. The men will come to the window when we're outside.

'You bastards, better take that rope aff, or yir gonna git it.'

Calum will open his jacket. 'What, this rope?'

Then we run like the wind as they slam the windows to come after us.

Full Moon is another one. There's a place called Brackens, at the back of St Mary's, and the house windows are nearly down to the floor, so we'd round up six or seven of us and bare our backsides and press them against the window and knock.

As the curtains open we'd bust into a chorus of 'Blue Moon, you saw me standing alone'.

I can't imagine what it must be like to open your curtains and see seven bare arses staring back at you. I do apologise to anyone who's had to endure that sight as I'm not sure whether Calum ever cleaned his.

Chapter Twenty-Three

The Puppies

I've been playing football throughout my childhood and I've become quite a nifty player. Most people in Dundee are football mad, as there's nothing else to do except have a punch-up or play football. My school team has even reached the Dundee Schoolboys' Cup Final.

I play for the Lawside first team and we're due to play Morgan High in the final. I've scored a few goals in the rounds before and am playing well when we reach the final. The manager of our team is my Maths teacher, a big chubby man with glasses. I've always got on quite well with him and his is one of my favourite classes.

Me and a few of the lads get there early as all our families are in the stand at Tannadice, Dundee United's home pitch, and we get into the dressing room before the rest of the lads. Another lad and me pick up a strip and put a top on, but when the manager comes in, he puts us on the bench and never plays me at all in the game. Just because we put the top on. We get beaten 4–2 and I'm glad – that idiot has watched me score goals for the whole competition and left me out to make an example of me, for reasons only known to him.

I've never imagined another person could ever make me feel as bad as Dad does, but he's succeeded. I have always sworn that one day I will play at Tannadice because I hate being beaten, and the feeling I have on this day will probably stay with me forever, as this was to be my one chance to prove to Dad that I'm not a useless waste of time that should never have been born, as he reminds me time and time again, and to make him proud of me.

And that Maths teacher has taken that away from me. He did it out of some stupid principle, to discipline me for putting that top on, but it was way out of proportion. The punishment most certainly doesn't fit the crime and he ruins the biggest day of my life.

I'll never forgive him for that, ever!

Bonnie has now had her puppies and most of my free time is spent looking after them and her. There are six of them and they are absolutely beautiful. Dad says we should wait until they're ten weeks, then sell some and give some to people who already have their names down. Well, that's the plan, but then the fireworks start.

The Puppies

It's a Saturday night around four. I'm at St Kilda Park playing football with some of the lads. I hear a fire engine coming up the road and then another. They're coming past the park and turn up towards my street, St Nicholas Place.

Everybody starts chasing it to see where it's going, so I walk up behind them thinking nothing of it as I want to get back to the game. '*Charlie, it's your hoose!*' I hear one lad shout.

I take to my heels up the street and as I get there all the windows are blowing out. My first thought is the puppies and Bonnie. The firemen are smashing the front door in and the flames are now licking out of the top of the windows.

'Where's my dog?' I scream in a fireman's face. 'Is my dad still in there? Where's the puppies?'

The next minute I turn around and see Bonnie being held back by one of the neighbours. She's yelping and trying to run back into the house. Several people are holding different puppies in their hands.

'Is my dad still in there?'

I am praying that he is.

'Just stay back, son,' the fireman snaps. Then out of the smoke comes Dad with the last of the puppies, covered in black smoke with its little head limp, like it's dead. The fireman grabs the puppy from Dad.

'You fucking idiot, you could have been killed.'

Dad's bent over with his hands on his knees, coughing his lungs up, and the fireman is giving the puppy mouth to mouth. Then he puts an oxygen mask on it, and the little thing starts coughing.

I'm made up but at the same time secretly disappointed that Dad escaped. He's gone into that blazing house six times to save these little things! I am shocked. Such a horrible bastard has just done something that only a few people in the world would have done. Risked his own life for a few puppies. I don't know how chuffed he is later when he finds out it was one of the puppies that knocked the electric fire over to set the house up while he was at the shops.

Everything we own has been destroyed and he blames me later, as he says he's had to cancel his insurance policy to get some money to buy me school clothes. Forgive me if I don't shed a tear. I never asked to be brought into his fucked-up world.

After that day Dad is different – or maybe it's because I'm getting older and don't pay as much attention to what he says when he's drunk. We've moved back down to St Fillans Road again, but this time it's another three-bedroom semi. The council says he can move into it until the other one is fixed up again. But when the time comes to move back, he point blank refuses, as he likes where he is now. I think that's because it's closer to the shops and nobody has heard any beatings or screaming. It's a new place to beat me up without rousing suspicion.

We've sold or given away all the puppies. We name the last one Smokey as it nearly died of smoke inhalation. He's a cracker, but he's been left with a cough a bit like whooping cough for the rest of his little life, poor thing.

And then there's Bonnie – my Bonnie. It happens very suddenly, one summer's day.

We're up in this idyllic place in the mountains of Perthshire called Clunie Loch. We've pitched the tent in a secluded spot and there's a twenty-foot square of gravel leading into the water. I'm standing waist high in the water watching shoals of perch swim around my legs and marvelling at being free of the war zone of home. The sun is gleaming in the water and all is peaceful.

Bonnie's in season again. It's really hot and she's been lying under a tree to keep out of the sun. This guy's kid grabs her by the ears and I tell the man that she's in season, and to get his daughter away. As you know, when Bonnie's in season you have to be careful of her and I can see she's getting annoyed, but neither the man nor Dad takes the warning. They're both sitting drinking their beers and chewing the fat and don't pay any attention.

Bonnie never actually bites the girl; she just grabs her face with her big jaws as a warning to go away, as she did with my backside that day, only grazing the skin on her chin and forehead. But when the man leaves, Dad decides to batter her with a tree branch as she runs around yelping. Then he turns on me.

'That fucking mutt o' yours is getting put doon when we git hame.'

I spend the night in the tent praying that this is just one more of his idle threats.

It's the third week in July 1990 and school's nearly over for the year. The next day I've forgotten all about what Dad said he'd do to Bonnie – until the moment when I come home from school a few days later and let myself in the house.

There's an odd kind of silence when I walk in. Usually Bonnie bounds up, jumping up and licking me as she comes to greet me. I know she's still on heat so she may not be as affectionate as she usually is, but where is she? I search the house and then go out into the street shouting out, 'Bonnie, come here, girl!'

But she doesn't come and when Dad comes home I think he's looking shifty; when I ask him where Bonnie is he slurs and mutters something about giving her to a farmer while I was at school, because she bit the little girl.

The blood rushes up from my toes to the tips of my hair. As I stare at him swaying in his chair with that smirk on his face, I'm devastated, inconsolable, seething with rage. I run into my room and crash onto my the bed and burst into tears.

Tonight for once Dad leaves me alone. But all I can think of is Bonnie, my dog, my closest friend, the only creature who has ever shown me love, and now she's gone.

The next day is Saturday, the weekend, and the house seems so quiet. I cannot get used to the fact that Bonnie's not with me. The weekend drags on slowly, painfully, and over the next few weeks I have a strong feeling that there was no farmer and that the evil bastard has probably killed her and buried her somewhere. I have no way of proving it but a remark he makes a few months later seems to confirm that suspicion.

'That mutt finally got what she deserved,' I hear him mumble one drunken night.

The day Dad gives Bonnie away is, for me, the last day of my childhood. He has taken away my best friend, my companion and protector, who was always there for me through the long dark nights of torment. I try to imagine that if Bonnie is alive she's happy and free, and at least safe from any more of Dad's beatings. But in my heart I know she's gone, and I also know that the time for payback has arrived. And it's not long in coming.

Chapter Twenty-Four

Red Light on the Stereo

I've arrived back at about two minutes past eight and Dad is drinking again, hammered, really, really drunk.

'Where have yi been?' he starts questioning me. 'What have yi been doing?'

This goes on until three in the morning. He's getting drunker and drunker, drinking more and more vodka. I'm falling asleep, trying to keep myself on the ball in case he suddenly attacks, but he never does this particular night. It's strange, he never does anything. He just sits there and sits there and eventually dozes off, still holding his vodka.

I wait ten, fifteen minutes to make sure he's out, then finally go to bed and fall asleep.

The next minute I wake up and my head feels like it's being blown apart. As I start to come round it dawns on me that it's Dad – he's stamping on my face. My head is getting shoved into the bed and when I look up I can see him stamping on my face with both feet – he's wearing green and white trainers and I can see blood on the front of them – and he's shouting '*Raaaaaaghhh!*' – really loud. He keeps slipping off me and falling and then getting up and doing it again.

And then I come to myself as I'm just out of sleep and he says, 'Just checking yi were awake, son!' and then walks back out of the room, leaving me there with blood pissing out of my nose.

What the fuck was that? I think.

This happens a few times. He usually kicks me once in the face and walks out – but on this particular occasion he jumps all over my head. I think he's less prepared to attack me when I'm up and awake and dressed, as by now I'm fifteen years old and I'm bigger and stronger, especially since I've been doing the kick boxing. Jumping on my head while I'm in bed is a much safer bet.

Maybe he knows the day's fast approaching when the tables will turn, when he'll get back from me what he's deserved all these years, and he's having a final fling while he has the strength to do it.

If so, his instincts are correct.

It's about four months away from my sixteenth birthday. I'm always looking forward to being sixteen as that is the day Dad will have no more control over me.

On this particular night I have been around at a place called Brackens Park. It's just another play park where we all go to light fires and have a few cans of beer.

I've started having a couple of cans in the evening with my mates as I'm now fifteen, and my age group and friends drink regularly, evenings and weekends. But I am never a big drinker as I've seen what it can do to you first hand – and I don't want to end up like Dad.

I'm always the joke-teller, the one with all the funny stories, even though in my head I'm a bomb waiting to go off. I now have to be home by ten – Dad's curfew has increased by an hour, probably so he can get smashed in peace a bit longer before he tries to smash into me – but I've drunk more than usual, three cans of Carlsberg and two bottles of Beck's. Even so, although I'm a bit tipsy, I'm not pissed like everyone else.

I look at my watch at 10.05 and remember that it's about a seven-minute walk back to St Fillans Road so I say my good-byes and head home, thinking of what he's going to say when I get back in. But I'm no longer scared. I think Dutch courage has taken over.

I walk in and Dad's sitting swaying in his normal position with a voddy in his hand, playing Extreme's 'More than Words' on the stereo and singing along to it as he often does. I can't believe that this man is my father. I'm now at the age where I should be meeting girls, and having friends coming to the house, but this scar-faced drunk gives them abuse or cries to crap songs in front of them. He's always listening to sentimental pop songs and singing at the top of his voice, sometimes dancing if he's mega pissed.

I sit down on the settee as he doesn't even see me come in. Then he turns around and looks at me with that stare I've seen for the past fifteen years. He then looks at his watch, stands up and turns the music off and then sits back on his two-seater, taking another drink of his hooligan soup – that's voddy to you and me.

'War the fuck iv you been?' he says.

I can feel my blood come up from the tips of my toes, right through my body and up my neck into my hair. 'What time di yi call this?' he slurs again.

I keep watching the red light on the stereo, not looking at him, as I know I'm about to flip.

'Ohy bastard,' I reply, using language and a tone he's never heard before. 'HALF FUCKIN' TEN! That's what time it is.'

'What did yi say?'

'You heard, you prick!'

I keep looking at the red light on the stereo, waiting for it to go green so I can erupt like a volcano.

'Did you jist fuckin' swear?' he says, standing up.

I never look at him, just the red light on the stereo.

'If you fucking touch me the night,' I say, 'it'll be the last time you touch anybody.'

I then turn and look at him, straight in the eyes, and stand up really quick. Even though he's drunk, I think he can see that I'm not joking. His expression has changed from aggression to friendly, as he puts his hand out as if to shake mine.

'Sorry, son,' he says. 'No hard feelings.'

I know what he's up to, so I play his little game.

'Nae bather, Dad.'

I put my right hand in his then *swing*, he tries to punch me with his other hand, but I move my head back then pull his hand that I've now locked mine into towards me, smashing my head into his face.

'Aggrr yi bastard! How does it feel, yi prick!' I roar as he falls backwards onto the two-seater sofa where I now start my ten-minute assault.

I'm shouting things at him as I stamp on his face with both feet. 'Do you remember biting me, tough guy? Do you remember bursting my ear drum?'

I slap him in the ear to try and burst his eardrum, as he did to me a few years ago. He's screaming like a woman, '*I can't hear! I can't hear!*'

I don't care; these ten minutes are nothing compared to the twelve-hour sessions I've had to endure throughout my childhood.

But pretty soon I know he's all right and I haven't broken his eardrum and he can hear perfectly well, as he changes tack. He now wants me to feel sorry for him.

'I know I've been a horrible dad to yi,' he says, 'but I'm dyin', son.'

Now he's wheedling for my sympathy and talking in this pathetic tone of voice just like Albert, the old geezer in *Steptoe and Son*, but I'm not prepared to play this game.

'Listen,' I say, 'I couldn't give a shit. You're not going to fucking turn this around. You want me to feel sorry for you?'

'I'm just tellin' yi, that's all. I'm dyin'.'

'Well good luck to you. If you're fucking drinking yourself to death, you've only got yourself to blame.'

'Yi ken what yi're granddad was like with me—'

'I couldn't give a shit. If I ever have kids I'd never hit them. You hit gran, you nearly battered my mum to death, you nearly killed me, you turned my childhood into a living hell, and you want me to feel sorry for you because you're drinking yourself to death? You're just nothing and the quicker you do that the better. I couldn't really care less if you died or not.'

'Ah well, you've got the right to say that, son.'

That's it. I'd had enough. I walk out.

Over the last two or three years I've rehearsed this moment in my mind many, many times. I've planned to replicate every single thing he has done to me over the years, and to give him the whole lot in one night. I've wanted to kill him, as I have been preparing myself for going to prison for a couple of years now. I've been thinking of sticking a knife in his heart and pouring a kettle of boiling water over his face when he was sleeping. It's never the thought of jail that has stopped me – it's the thought of him waking up and catching me on the way into the living room.

The Nipper

As I told you, I nearly did kill him when I was twelve, so I'm very confused now as to why I'm holding back, compared to what I've planned for him in my head, as he's relatively weak and really drunk.

Well, for one thing, biting is not my style. I'm not an animal like him. The punches I give him are actually fairly half-hearted: even though I'm wound up I can still control myself. So you could say I've stored up more anger by not letting go on him.

But even though it isn't who I want to become, I guess it's inevitable – I have walked outside and left Dad lying on the sofa in the same position he used to leave me, and knocked on the neighbour's door and told them he might need an ambulance.

I'm sitting on the fence outside my house, contemplating my next move, wondering if I should go back in and finish him off or wait for the police to come and have a go at them, as my blood is now pumping.

But inside I'm feeling completely numb. No fear, no panic, nothing. Then I look down at my fingers and see that my hands are shaking and I start to realise that my whole body is trembling.

It's then that it hits me. The nightmare is over. The nightmare that began when I saw him, or dreamt I saw him, dragging my mum around the room by her hair, the nightmare that came alive when I became the object that was dragged around the room – for years and years and years.

And now it's finally ended. I'm free of Dad and that hell-hole. I hardly register the fact that I'm sobbing and crying as I decide to give Mum a ring, tell her what's happened and ask her what I should do next, as she's the one person who's hated him as much as I do.

'Hi, Mum, it's Charlie.'

'Hi son, what ir yi up ti?'

'I've just done mi dad in.'

'Brilliant son,' she says, without hesitation. 'Good lad, you can come and live over here.'

She's really excited because she's wanted me to come back and live with her for years, and she's been waiting so long for this day to come. She's tried many many times to say to Dad that if he couldn't cope, she'd have me, but he's always refused point blank – 'Fuck off, yi'll never get Charlie' – or ignored or stonewalled her. But I only find that out after this phone call.

'Just leave yir stuff and come straight here. We can get it later.'

Suddenly a huge weight has been lifted off my shoulders. I will be able to live a normal life. I've seen those movies in which prisoners finally get to walk out of the prison gates at the end of their term, but I never thought it would happen to me.

I'm so looking forward to living with Tommy and Bobby, as we've become really close in the times that we've visited each other. I haven't really got to know Bobby well before this time as Dad didn't want to have anything to do with him because he wasn't his son, but during the last few months we've started to get to know each other – he's quickly becoming the younger brother I've never had and we're bonding like never before.

A fresh start is just what I need. A new life – away from the torture den.

When I move to Mum's in Mill o'Mains, three miles away, I think it's going be really hard, as I have to leave behind all the mates I have grown up with and moving to a new area is always a nightmare. Making friends, getting used to your surroundings and sharing a room with someone else – in other words, my big brother Tommy.

For the first few days I keep expecting there will be repercussions. Every time the phone rings I think it must be the police. I have visions of them arriving at Mum's front door and taking me to the station for questioning. I see myself being forced into the back of a paddywagon, a hand pressed down on my head, followed by hours and hours of interrogation, just like Dad always subjected me to.

But it's weird. Nothing happens at all. After about a week it dawns on me that there will be no comeback. It's like I've had a toothache all my life and it's suddenly gone. And then it occurs to me that there were never any repercussions all those years that Dad battered and tortured me – no one ever reported him: he virtually got away with murder, so why would I imagine that my ten minutes of payback would land me in any kind of trouble?

And that's when it hits me and I realise that I could have left to live with Mum years ago – ever since I got back in touch with her – and he wouldn't have been able to do anything about it. He couldn't snatch me back like he did when I was a two year old, and already I'm regretting the time that I've lost, the years that I've wasted being a prisoner of my fear.

As for Dad, I think he must know now that the game's up, as far as he and I are concerned. He's hardly going to press charges against me, not after all those years when I was his punchbag. He must know he can't come after me, he must know that what I gave him was just a drop in the ocean of pain he inflicted on me over the years, and that I can easily deal out far more punishment if given the opportunity.

Occasionally I wonder, *Who's Dad gonna batter now?* and I find out later that he's met another woman – but she leaves after the first time he hits her. Clever move, love.

About a week after the Final Showdown he rings me at Mum's.

'That's me and you finished,' he says. 'I can't believe you did that to me.'

'What! Are you fucking taking the piss?' I explode.

There's no shame, no remorse, not even any acknowledgement from him that he deserved it. Nothing. I'm the one who's done something wrong as far as he's concerned and therefore we should never speak again. Well, that suits me fine. It suits me down to the ground. He's out of my life and that's the way I want it to stay.

My whole world seems to be turning around; things are totally different at Mum's. We have regular meals – breakfast, lunch and tea.

'Slow down, son,' Mum will say to me again, just like she did when I was eight. 'It's like you've never seen food before.'

It's the same old story. There were so many nights back at Dad's that I never ate because if I got beaten early on before tea, ten hours later I just wanted to get to bed and catch some sleep. But this time I'm eating out of sheer joy. I'm alive and free!

I have never had so much sleep in my life than when I move to Mum's. It's like a luxury holiday – or what I imagine a luxury holiday might feel like.

And every minute, every second of the day I have to remind myself, I'm free – I'm finally free of that evil psychopath.

But the real truth is, I'm just about as free of Dad as a Dundee summer is from the snows of winter.

Chapter Twenty-Five

Off the Leash

I establish a new routine living at Mum's. I start at a new school, Morgan Academy, although I'm not there for very long – only a month – but then again I wasn't at Lawside half the time. I don't know anybody and the only people who speak to me are friends of Tommy's as we're practically identical at this point. So I finally tell Mum there's no point in my being there. I don't even bother to say anything to any of the teachers. I just stop going. I leave school with no qualifications and no expectations, but I don't care now as I'm free of *him*.

In any case I'd much rather find a job – any job – and be out in the real world.

I'm sixteen and have never really acquired any skills or a trade. I play football a lot and have fixed a few roofs and swept a few chimneys with Dad, but skills-wise I'm practically useless. But as I'm bright, enthusiastic and have the gift of the gab, I soon get a job in a joke-cum-fancy-dress-hire shop in Dundee City centre. It starts as just Saturdays and soon turns full-time which suits me down to the ground. I'm in charge of hiring the costumes out and keeping an eye out for thieves, as I know most of them.

Since living with Mum, Bobby and I have started going to an under-eighteens disco called Buddies in Braughty Ferry, a posh area outside Dundee. I didn't know I had a sense of rhythm as I'd never danced before or even been near a club. I expect I've got it from Gran who, you may recall, was a professional dancer in the Pally in Dundee years ago. But when I get out onto Buddies' dance floor, I discover I can simply close my eyes and my body moves of its own accord. I feel like I'm somewhere up in the sky amongst the clouds with music blasting down from heaven – like God's having a rave and has only invited me.

Wee Bobby's a brilliant dancer as well, and we're quickly making up our own moves: from the minute we walk into Buddies until the last song we're stuck to the dance floor. We make up dances like playing golf, basketball, picking berries, stamping our feet, walking around the whole club, while loads of other people follow us, a bit like a conga line, stamping their feet. I feel like the Pied Piper. It's amazing, people are friendly, and I've quickly become the centre of attention. It's as if I've finally found my reason for being born.

There's one girl who's like a female version of me – but only in a dance sense: she's like a mermaid – long blonde curly hair, lovely skin and she has her own dress style. Well, she has style – she's from Broughty Ferry, the posh area where Dad asked for hot water and a teabag. We end up dance partners for about a year and I never ask her out in case it ruins the thing that we have, as dancing is now more important to me than anything. It's like that relationship John Travolta has with his dancing partner in *Saturday Night Fever* – apart of course from the white suit!

I'm starting to win all the competitions in Dundee. There's Buddies, Fat Sam's and the Coconut Grove, a massive club that stages competitions for young people all over the East Coast. It seems like I've sorted out all the bottled-up anger and aggression and moved on from the trauma of my childhood. But that's very far from the truth: I haven't really moved on at all, nor have I got over it. I've simply blanked it out, locked it away deep down inside me. It's hardly surprising. I'm finally physically free of Dad and my life with him, and the last thing I want to do is think about him or what he did to me. I just want to make up for lost time – the joy, fun, freedom and good times.

Since leaving Dad I've put him out of my mind, but now that I'm winning all these competitions I keep getting this urge to let him know, just like when I wanted him to be proud of me playing for the Lawside first team at Tannadice that time when my Maths teacher robbed me of the chance. Finally, on impulse, I go and see him.

He acts like he's doing me a huge favour letting me in the house and when I finally tell him that I've won a dance competition at the Coconut Grove – I'm third best in Scotland in the Under-16s – he doesn't even sneer about it, he simply turns it round to him.

'Ah, yi got that off me!'

Even now he still won't give me credit for making something of myself and I realise that even if I had scored the winning goal that day at Tannadice it wouldn't have made any difference because his life was all about him.

This is my first visit to him since the Final Showdown – and, as it turns out, the last for many, many years. But Tommy goes to see him again – and it's one visit that Tommy later tells me Dad won't forget in a hurry. And it happens as a result of my falling asleep at a party.

During the time I'm living at Mum's Tommy's introducing me to his circle of friends and I'm adjusting to normal life, away from Dad. One night we go to a party at the house of one of Tommy's friends. After a fantastic evening I fall asleep sitting up on the arm of a chair. Around ten o'clock everyone decides to go into town to continue the party but Tommy doesn't want to leave me so he asks one of his friends to wake me up.

I open my eyes to see fifteen people staring at the floor trying not to look at me and I have no idea why. I then hear Tommy shouting, 'That fucking bastard, I'm going to kill him!' and then the front door slams. I have no idea what's happened as three of his friends run after him.

246

Later, on the way into town in a taxi, someone tells me the truth. When they were trying to wake me up and my eyes were still closed, I put my hands up to defend myself and I was shouting in terror, 'No, Dad, please, no Dad!'

My reaction told Tommy and his friends everything they needed to know about Dad and what he'd done to me. Of course I'm embarrassed and humiliated that I have been exposed in this way. And even though I've had my revenge on Dad it brings it home to me how mentally damaged and traumatised I still am.

As for Tommy, fortunately for him, two or three of his friends have persuaded him not to go straight round to Dad's house as he would have certainly killed him at this point. Even so his anger still festers and although it's weeks later, he does go round to Dad's house and the battering he gives him leaves Dad unrecognisable immediately afterwards, just as it had left me on many occasions. But I no longer care whether Dad's beaten up or not. The damage has been done and he's now out of my life.

After that, if he ever does cross my mind, it's like a distant memory of a nightmare which I'd rather forget. But if I really think I've got him out of my head and flushed away all the damage he's done to me over the years, I'm fooling myself.

I'm getting a lot of people coming up to me saying, 'Alright Tommo, how's things?' People in town call me Tommo and women sit on my knee in the middle of a club when I've never even met them before.

'Alright Tommo, I've not seen you since school.'

Tommo's my older brother Tommy's nickname. Although he's two years older than me, we look so alike that people who've known him for eighteen years can't tell the difference. None of us in the family can see it but everyone else says we look like twins. He's even fallen out with his girlfriend because two girls run up to him in town and squirt him in the face with pump-action water pistols.

'That's for not speaking to us in Buddies.' Then they run off and leave him to explain what he's been doing in an under-eighteens nightclub. He's in the doghouse until he introduces me to her one day. I walk out from behind her when they're talking.

'Jesus Christ, there's two of them,' she gasps, accidentally spitting her can of Coke all over me.

When Buddies isn't on I go into town with Tommy to all the over-eighteen pubs. He knows all the doormen and we get in everywhere, no problem. We just hate the fact that Bobby's too young to come with us, and so does he.

'I canna wait till I'm sixteen. This is a load o' shite.'

He's the only one that can get away with swearing in front of Mum as he's invented codewords in case he gets caught. He'll say things like 'Shut yir fucking puss' really quickly and Mum will shout, 'What did you just say?'

'I'm just telling Charlie he should have got the bus.'

Bobby has me in stitches. He has this mad giggle, 'Teehee teehee' and there'll be slavers running down his chin and bubbles coming out of his nose. He'll say stuff under his breath to Mum and then go into fits of laughter if she catches him. Mum just laughs at him, as he'll have Tommy and me on the floor pissing our sides.

Bobby is funny and really good-natured, although if you wind him up, he can blow – and Tommy knows exactly what buttons to push. One Christmas Mum gets Bobby a six by three foot snooker table. We're all having a laugh playing each other at Winner Stays On in the living room. Bobby's just beaten Tommy and I'm on next, but Tommy can't resist winding him up, as brothers do. He keeps lifting the table leg when Bobby's taking his shot and all the balls keep rolling down one side of the table.

'Stop it, yi dick,' Bobby snarls.

Tommy's drinking a can of beer as we're going into town later in the evening and he's decided to have a couple before we go. Bobby's a bit wound up that he can't go so now's probably not the best time to push his buttons. But Tommy lifts the table leg again.

'Mum, you better tell him ti fuckin' stop it.'

He's obviously ready to pop.

'Right, Tommy,' says Mum. 'Stop annoying 'im, that's enough.'

Tommy leans back to take a drink from his can after making faces at him behind Mum's back when all of a sudden, *whack*, the beer goes everywhere. Bobby has swung his snooker cue straight into Tommy's face.

'You little bastard,' he shouts.

Mum jumps in the middle and Bobby's now standing laughing, 'Ha, yi never seen that coming did yi!'

'I'll get yi back fir that, yi wee prick.'

I'm now laughing at his face, as Bobby looks really smug with his snooker cue still held like a baseball bat. If Tommy wasn't drinking his can at that point, I think his new nickname would have been 'Gummy!'

Tommy sits back down and half laughs. 'There's sumin' rang wi you, di yi ken that? There's sumin' rang wi your can,' he says, bursting into tears of laughter.

I always get on well with both of them but they're always at each other. It must have been living together all those years. I try to spend equal amounts of time with each of them, but with Bobby being younger, Tommy and I are together a lot more.

After all, Buddies is only open once a week, and the pubs and clubs are every night.

After nine months or so of staying at Mum's, I'm beginning to crave my own space as me and Tommy are becoming young men and privacy is non-existent with two people in a room. I go down to the social and tell them I'm homeless so I can get my own place and some independence.

They set me up with a grotty little bedsit in a shit hole of an area with junkies for neighbours. Mum helps me – she scrubs the whole house, floorboards and all, with bleach and disinfectant and decorates the whole place as I don't have a clue how to hang wallpaper, and then adds a woman's touch with curtains and plants. We go to Dens Road Market, a massive indoor market in Dundee that sells secondhand everything. It's an Aladdin's Cave for tramps or for people that are skint. I get everything except the hall carpet.

From the moment I get that house my life is a rollercoaster. I'm going to raves as I love the music which is happy house. But they go on until seven in the morning and when you have a wild, obsessive streak like me, you don't want to leave the dance floor. It's the best place in the world for a lot of people, but not for me. By now I'm taking drugs as well as drinking. It starts with speed and I'm soon having everything that's going. The very worst thing a person in my mental state can do at this point is to add any more confusion to a brain that is already volatile and unstable.

Some mornings I wake up, and my hands are cut or broken. I look out of the window and cars will be smashed up in the street, with someone's wooden deckchair sticking out of a front windscreen. Other times I'll come to myself in a party full of blokes that I used to fight with as a kid and not have a clue how I got there, or why. And all the time I tell myself that I've escaped my past, not realising that I'm dragging it along behind me like a set of invisible chains.

Tommy, Bobby and me are inseparable. It's like we're trying to make up for all the years we were apart and for all of us the bad times and good times are mixed up together like a great big stew. And we do have great times together, like the night our three girlfriends, who are all in the Territorial Army, persuade us to sneak into their barracks.

I should have joined the army, as I could penetrate enemy lines undetected, no problem. I manage to escape capture twice, and when the women officers come to check on the girls, I'm hiding in a top bunk behind one of them who is only too happy to play along. Bobby, meanwhile, is trying to hide in a four-foot-high metal locker, while Tommy is squashed on the floor under a bed making loads of noise, and it's becoming a game of cat and mouse between the army officers and us.

Suddenly the light goes on and the sound of laughter is deafening. I have to peek over this girl and see what's happening. Everyone's in stitches. As I look over her shoulder, to my amazement I see a white sheet in the middle of the floor standing, like a ghost. One of my two nutter brothers is obviously under it.

I lay my head back down, because if I start laughing I won't be able to stop.

'How did you find me?' Tommy blurts out as the officer lifts the sheet. Well, stick a fork in me, I'm done. I get up from behind the girl, howling with laughter.

'Where the hell did you come from?'

Bobby comes out of hiding as well.

'That's it, I'm calling the police.'

'Aright luv, calm doon, we're going this time. We're just lookin' fir him.' Bobby turns and points at me.

I'm standing there in my boxer shorts with my hair all over the place.

'You have two minutes to get your clothes on and get off these barracks, or I will call the police.'

We clear off sharpish as I'm already known to the police – we're still fighting every week, wrecking people's houses. Nothing phases us. Even when the police turn up we don't care and treat them just like another Dundee gang that we're fighting against. We're a law unto ourselves and all reality has gone out of the window. The anger that Dad has planted inside me is spiralling out of control. During this two-year period my criminal record goes from idiot charges – like breach of the peace, the odd punch-up in town and theft of a fan – into an increasingly violent stream of assaults. I know we're all heading for prison but it never seems to stop us. The only thing on my mind is to seek and destroy, and I think it's the same for Tommy and Bobby.

In all my battles throughout this period I can never remember the faces of the people I fight with. All I can see is the face of my dad, Evil Jock. Every memory I have seems to go back to his face, that night I hit him back. Right through to the date of writing this, if when someone's drunk they get a bit nasty, all I can see is Dad's features coming through their face.

I'm building up a substantial portfolio in the police station and although I've managed to stay out of prison by the skin of my teeth, it's only a matter of time before the law catches up with me.

It's early February 1997 and I'm in court for fighting in town, expecting another fine or probation. I'm sitting in the dock, thinking about what club to go to that night, and then I realise the guy's talking to me.

'The courts have given you ample warning about your behaviour. You seem to think you can go around doing as you please.'

I'm paying attention now, as no judge has ever spoken directly to me before.

'I have no option but to remand you in custody for three months. Take him down.'

Chapter Twenty-Six

Heartache Following Me

A short while later I'm released from Perth Prison. Once out of the prison grounds and breathing in the fresh air, it dawns on me how sweet fresh air is. It's early March and spring in Dundee is like winter everywhere else, but to me at this moment it's like summer. I even imagine I can feel the sun on my face but of course it's only the usual Dundee smog.

Even so it feels good to be alive and free. And getting out of this place reminds me of the day I walked out of Dad's house for the last time – although of course I was in a much greater state of shock that time as my previous prison sentence had been so much longer. With time off for good behaviour I'd been incarcerated with that bastard for almost sixteen years.

Mum's split up with her third husband by this time. I think Dale just wanted a quiet life; it was all too hectic with three noisy lads there, and now Mum's on her own again. As for me, I'm twenty-one with no job and no plans for the future, and to be honest, I've had enough. I have to get away from Dundee – and Spain seems like the answer. I tell Mum, Tommy and Bobby I'm leaving, sort out my passport and flight, and then I'm off.

Adios amigo, una grande cervesa por favor. Charli-eo is off-io, as my old pal Calum Patterson might say.

Arriving in Benidorm in March the place is a ghost town, hardly anywhere is open and the weather's worse than Scotland. I go into a bar and have a drink and stumble across a karaoke bar around the corner. There's a lot more people in there, but I don't care as I'm just exploring on my own, taking everything in. I go from place to place, having a drink in every bar I go into, sometimes two.

The following morning I wake up with this bright light in my eyes, like I'm on an operating table. My head feels like it's in a vice. I open my eyes and the most beautiful picture is in front of me. It's morning and I'm lying on the beach under an umbrella, beside a sun lounger – not on it – with the sun beating down on my face. I've never been anywhere so beautiful. This is my heaven.

I get up off the sand, dust myself down and start walking along the beach with boots, jeans and a jacket on from the night before. I think the storm has cleared the air as it's boiling. Well, to me it is as I've just moved from Fridgeland.

I have a theory about Scotland: the reason it has so much crime and domestic violence is because the place is like a fridge freezer and nobody wants to go outside. The ones that do go out tend to have a punch-up to keep warm. Whoever invented Scottish weather has a very sick sense of humour.

Back in town I'm staggering a bit, and have to close one eye to focus on the road ahead, mainly because I'm tired from walking around all day and night – but also, of course, because I'm a little pissed. I can see two lads on the other side of the road walking up towards me. It sounds like they're arguing. As they come closer I notice that one of them has his shirt ripped open and there's blood all down his mouth and chest. I should just walk past but Good Samaritan Charlie decides to check if they're OK.

'Are yi aright mate?'

'Do I look fuckin' alright?'

'What happened?'

'Fuck off, you Scotch twat,' he says in a strong Welsh accent.

'Nae wonder yir face is like that, yi cheeky cunt.' I carry on walking down towards the beach.

'Oi, arsehole, come back 'ere and say that.'

They've started to cross the road and walk down behind me. I can feel my blood boil at the fact that there's two of them. If that bloke was on his own, I know I would have ignored him, but as I hate any kind of bullying, two against one like this will always get to me. I keep walking at first.

'Yeah keep walking, you shitbag,' the other one says, laughing with his mate. Then a bottle smashes on the ground just past me.

I stop walking and turn around.

'Aright tough guy, let's go.' I start walking back up the middle of the road towards them. One of them, the bloke with his face still intact, starts bouncing in the middle of the road twenty yards away from me.

'You picked the wrong lads to have a go at, boyo,' he says.

I just keep walking towards them, getting more and more angry as he talks tactics – or rather hurls them – at his mate. 'I'll put him down and you stamp his face in.'

I'm thinking, *you pair of idiots*, and I'm having flashbacks about beating Dad up. As I get closer, they look a lot bigger than I first thought, but that's good, I won't feel so bad for what I'm about to do. I sweep the first guy's legs from underneath him, and the other one rugby tackles me into a parked car. I hardly know what I'm doing by this time as it's almost like an out-of-body experience. All I know is I'm breathing heavily and as we spill around a corner against a big glass hotel room window, flashbacks of St Fillans Road fly through my head.

Then he starts screaming at the top of his voice. 'I've had enough, I've had enough.'

I suddenly snap out of it, realising that it isn't Dad. Then I stop and sit down on the bonnet of a parked car, and can't believe what I have been doing. We both have blood all over us and he's sitting on the ground with his back against the wall.

'That's enough, Jock. That's enough, mate. Let's just forget about it.'

I am confused. 'Did you just call me "Jock"?' Does he know my father? Can he see him in me? My head's now all over the place.

'I didn't mean anything by it.' He thinks I'm offended with the Jock comment because I'm Scottish.

'Let me gee yi a hand,' I say.

He's panting and so am I, as I go over to give him a hand up. But as I do, the bloke that's on the ground around the corner has got up, and can't see where we've gone at first, but then he finds us. I don't see him coming. While I'm helping his friend off the floor he comes at me from behind. *Crash!* He has rugby-tackled me straight through a plate-glass apartment window. We're now lying on a bedroom floor covered in glass, and then he staggers up and runs off with his friend.

I'm glad they've gone as I'm exhausted. They must have been rugby players. I can't believe it – there are hardly any holidaymakers here, I'm on my own, starting a new life and I still manage to get in a fight.

It's like that old song, *I look around and there's a heartache following me*, only in my case it's my demons, my dad, that's following me.

I sit on the end of the bed catching my breath and trying to clean the blood and check for any major glass wounds. I'll be OK, though, it's nothing I've not had before.

The next thing I know I'm lying face down on the bed, handcuffed, with a gun at my head, with someone screaming at me from two inches away in Spanish.

It's the police. I must have fallen sleep on the bed. I can't understand a word they're saying and they can't understand me. Even if they did speak English I don't think they'd have got my lingo at the time, as my Dundonian accent is very strong. They drag me into the police car, put me in jail for three days and feed me on thin slices of pepperoni on a baguette that's more like a house brick than a roll.

How have I managed it? Yet again I'm in trouble with the law. Whatever went on when I was a kid, I still want to keep telling myself that it doesn't bother me any more. I'm a happy-go-lucky person. I make people laugh. I'm always the life and soul of the party. So why do I still have this burning desire to destroy people? Why does everyone want to have a go at me? At least that's the way it seems to me at this time.

I start thinking about Dad and what he used to do to me and suddenly I'm a three-year-old kid, frightened, alone, lying on the bed, bawling my eyes out. Although I physically left Dad behind the night of our showdown in St Filland Road, he still has a stranglehold on my soul. Every brick of the wall I have built up round myself has the name 'Jock' stamped on it and I know it's something in myself I'll have to change as nobody else is going to help me.

So much for my new start, my new dreams, my new hopes, my new life …

Chapter Twenty-Seven

A Voice in the Wilderness, a Face in the Crowd

*B*y April Benidorm has turned from a ghost town into a never-ending party. I get a job as a dancer and though it's only one night a week, it's more money in my pocket and I'm feeling better about my life. My anger is subsiding, or at least being locked up again. I'm still drinking every night but my body is not receiving the same punishment I've been giving it for the past four years.

Bobby decides to join me in Spain as he feels the same about Dundee as I do. I've got him a job as a doorman after a couple of weeks and he's having a ball.

Then one day, out of the blue, something extraordinary happens. I meet Sophie Jones, one of the most beautiful creatures on God's earth.

The first time I see her I pick her up over my shoulder and take her into the club that I work for. I do this with anyone who tries to walk past, as you get money for each person that comes in. I've met some really nice-looking girls over the summer and seen a lot of stunners but Sophie is in a league of her own. She has long blonde hair, brown/hazel eyes, is really tall and slim, tanned and politely spoken, and I have a funny feeling she's been sent down to me from heaven.

She has this green dress on, very short, just below her backside, and legs that seem to go on forever. What's more I click with her straight away. She's different to all the other girls I normally come into contact with. I know that she's special, a class apart, and I've never expected to meet anyone like her.

It's three in the morning and we're both still in the club. She looks over and I'm dancing with a palm tree. So even if I can't say for sure whether I've swept her off her feet, I've certainly had an impact on the palm tree.

At this stage in my life, although I have always been searching, I always thought I was destined to be a loner. I don't want to be a loner but I never thought in a million years that I would find anyone, even though I'm desperately looking for someone to trust.

My natural reaction to anyone who ever shows me any love or affection is to back off. I still remember how Dad would tell me he loved me and do me in on the same night. I won't let anyone get that close to me or mess with my head – which is all I have known when it comes to intimacy. The hand that fed me has been the hand that bit me and I've told myself so many times that I won't be fooled again.

But something about Sophie throws me off guard. She sweeps under the radar. I'm not expecting someone like her to come into my life and it knocks me sideways.

I spend every day of the two weeks of her holiday with her. Bobby has met Katie, one of her friends who is one half of a pair of twins. It's a great release for me to be spending time with someone so genuine and honest and innocent. Sophie's only three years younger than I am, but I seem much older as I've had to grow up fast.

The day she's meant to go home to Cheshire, she cries because her father has told her she can't stay and get a job. This girl is more impulsive than I am, I think to myself. I'm pretty gutted when she goes home, as I'm getting used to seeing her every day and I actually miss her. I've never had that feeling before about anyone as I've always been a bit of a loner. I like my own company but Sophie Jones – she is a light in a dark room.

She heads back home and almost immediately I am missing her badly as it's suddenly dawned on me that she has been the only good thing in my life. I cope with this in the usual way I always cope with problems. I go back to my crazy world and take more drugs and fill myself with more booze to forget. I have started to become really close to a group of lads from Algeria. They've taken me under their wing as one of their own. We teach each other Scottish and Algerian football songs, and laugh about things we've done in the past. They are the nicest people you could meet, but if you get on the wrong side of them, it's a different story.

I feel quite safe though, as I'm like a brother to them. I have met some seriously disturbed characters over the years and people that are known as gangsters, but these lads are basically trained killers and in a league of their own. Some are ex-soldiers who have completed the compulsory two years in the army. Others have gone AWOL before joining, as they know it would mean they'd have to wipe out whole villages of their own friends and people. One lad, Jamal, has killed over thirty people while in the army and has never batted an eyelid.

They never boast about these experiences. We just sit and chat, swapping stories about our lives. Then one day when I'm dining with them in one of their houses, I walk into the kitchen for a glass of water and see two black 9 mm handguns sitting on the worktop. Instantly I realise that they must be involved in something that's way over my head.

With Sophie gone I'm back on drugs again, doing things that only a man high on cocaine would even dream of. As I grew up I always had a cut-off switch, and could stop when I knew something was a bit too much. But that switch has now gone.

As part of my initiation into their group I agree to go on the back of a motorbike, get dropped off behind a building where some Spanish guy works, wait until he comes out, then stab him in the arse as he owes the Algerians a lot of money.

Jamal goes over exactly where to hit the guy and what to say as I do it. 'You push the knife in his left ass cheek, straight in the middle.'

He's standing up in front of me, pointing at the area I have to go for. 'This area is safe, there's no main artery, it is just muscle.'

'What if he moves and it goes in the right cheek?'

'Fuck him, he shouldn't have moved. It's his own fault. If he'd paid my money he would have no problems with his ass. After you do it, he'll fall to the floor. All you say is *dos million pesetas!* Then you walk away.'

I work it out, the bloke owes him £10,000, but I never ask what it's for as it's really none of my business. I'm just there to carry out orders.

I leave the house and jump on the back of a motorbike with another lad, putting a seven-inch lock knife I've been given into my inside pocket, then we're off – on a military mission to search and destroy. As the bike tears through the back streets of Benidorm, I'm mulling things over in my head as warm air blows into my face. I don't really feel any emotion or fear as the drugs I've taken to psyche myself up have clouded my thoughts, convincing myself that this guy deserves what he's about to receive.

After ten minutes we arrive at a car park behind some apartments in the middle of nowhere. It's pitch black as it's about one in the morning and the place looks deserted.

'OK, I'll be over there. When you have done it, get here quickly.' He points to a dark street between two apartment blocks that are only half built. I have already been given my instructions – what he looks like, what time he finishes work, and so on.

I'm on my own from here on in, dressed like a cat burglar and high as a kite.

I calmly walk into the car park and crouch down behind a bin shelter, between two parked cars, thinking which way I'm going to run and what to say, going over it in my head so I don't make any mistakes. Talking to myself, as my heart starts pumping.

'In the left cheek, *dos million pesetas*.'

Then I started having doubts and qualms.

What if I miss his arse and hit a main artery by mistake and kill him? What if he has kids?

It seems even the evil voices in my head that used to make me snap are having second thoughts. I have turned into two different people, two voices arguing with each other.

What if you kill him?

Fuck him, stick it in his back!

This goes on for around fifteen minutes and there's still no sign of him. All of a sudden a door opens at the back of a restaurant next door to the flats. Someone comes out and walks into the car park, passing the car I'm now crouched behind. It's definitely the bloke.

I take the knife out of my inside pocket and walk up behind him, ready to do what I've gone there to do. Then I stop.

I've had a vision of Dad. And instead of it fuelling my rage, the licence to kill, I suddenly begin to wonder if I'm becoming Jock. An unstable maniac with a chemical imbalance or a self-inflicted drugged-up thug that wants revenge against a world that has done nothing against him. At this moment I'm two different people, one of whom I'm seriously starting to dislike.

I'm standing in the middle of the car park with the knife by my side only feet from the guy, shocked at what I've nearly done. The good voice in my head has overpowered the evil one that wanted me to kill him. It's like being in a film – it never seems real. The lad has now turned around as he must have heard my footsteps behind him. He looks at me, then his eyes look down towards the knife.

'*Dos million pesetas*.'

I can see by the look on his face that he's petrified.

'*Sí, mañana*,' he says as he takes off into the darkness.

I just can't do it. All the way back to the getaway bike I keep thinking I can't believe I was about to stab someone who's never done anything to me.

'Did you get him?'

'No, he seen me and ran into a car, but your money is on its way.'

'Did you say what I told you to say?'

'Yep, he'll bring it tomorrow. Your money is on its way.'

We don't speak much on the way back to the house. He doesn't ask me what's gone on, as I've now promised him his money will be paid in the morning. I'm ninety-nine per cent sure after seeing the look on the lad's face in the car park. Well, I'm praying I've read his expression correctly.

Luckily for the bloke, the good side of me has the upper hand. Luckily for me, the next day, the bloke sends a woman to Jamal's house with the £10,000 he owes them. He must have seen the look in my eyes, the one that sometimes scares me when I look in the mirror.

The Algerians ask me what I said to him and why I didn't stab him but I just tell them, 'There's more than one way to skin a cat.'

Not that they care how I did it, they're just impressed at how quickly they got their money back. But I think it's fate that I've gone that night – fate giving the guy a helping hand – as I've seen a few of the not so fortunate people they've paid a visit to. And fate for me too, as I have this odd feeling of vertigo, like I've been standing on the edge of a cliff, ready to fall – and something has held me back.

I'm back from the brink, back in the real world, back on dry land. I don't want to be in that negative limbo land of drugtaking and violence; I don't want to be running all my life from a father whose anger has infected my mind and whose sickness has eaten into my soul; I don't want to see that blackness behind the eyes when I stare into the glass.

I want to be Good Charlie, whatever that means and whatever it takes.

*   *   *

After that night I know I have to change my ways and try to turn my life around yet again. I've been writing letters to Sophie since she moved back to England and she's started an Advertising course at Lancashire University in Preston. There's something about her I can't get out of my head, like she's been sent down to me from whoever's up there to save me from myself – like a kind of guardian angel – and she's the only one who can do it.

When her face flashes through my mind it makes me happy: it's like an oasis of calm and serenity in the turmoil of my life and I feel better about myself. Is it her innocence or am I idealising her and putting her on a pedestal? After all, she's not really an angel, she's just a human being, flesh and blood like me. But she seems so nice and friendly compared with some of the people in my life.

I have to move on from Spain, as it clearly isn't helping at all. I decide to go back to see Sophie in Preston, to see if it really was just a holiday romance or something stronger. I still don't trust myself and think that maybe my mind wasn't operating rationally the last time I saw her, and Bobby wants to come with me see his girlfriend Katie.

I haven't told Sophie we're coming, as Bobby and I want to surprise her and Katie. Armed only with an address of some student halls in Preston, we board a train and set off on the journey. On the train I start worrying that maybe she's met someone else or has gone home to Cheshire for a holiday, or even worse, given me the wrong address. But Bobby reminds me that we've been writing to each other and it's obviously the real address.

When we arrive at the student halls Sophie isn't there. Someone on the intercom buzzes me in when I explain who I am. Sophie has been telling all her student friends about me – brilliant.

I leave my bags there, and Bobby goes off to see the twins in the next block and I go for a walk outside to calm myself down, as I'm getting really excited about seeing her again. Bobby comes back out from the other block and we decide to go for a beer in a pub near the halls. I only have one drink, just to calm my nerves, then have a game of pool, thinking about what I'm going to say to her. Then we walk back half an hour later to see if she's come home. I press the intercom.

'Hello, is Sophie home yet? It's Charlie.'

'Hi! It's me,' comes a familiar voice. 'I'm coming down now.'

My heart is pounding and Bobby keeps ruffling my hair up, trying to make me look a mess while giggling in that mad way he has. The door opens and there she is, looking even better than I've remembered. I must have dreamt about this moment.

I still can't believe it's Sophie, or that she could really be pleased to see me.

But I can't mistake that look on her face. I can see she's deliriously happy to see me. We grab each other really tight and kiss. It feels unbelievable to be back with the only person on the planet I've ever had a serious connection with. There's something about her, the way she looks at me, that smile that would light up a room, her infectious laugh and her honest eyes.

That's what I've thought about all this time. How honest her eyes are.

We stay in Preston for three months, Bobby with Katie, me with Sophie. Bobby and I get jobs in Southport at Pontin's Holiday Camp – not as Red Coats but as builders. The place is having a revamp and they need people to demolish it.

Travelling is a nightmare every day, and Sophie only has a tiny room in the halls with a shared kitchen and toilet. It's cramped and I'm not used to sleeping next to anyone, especially in a single bed. But the boss of the building company we work for has some chalets on site that aren't being used so we move into them and the girls sneak up at weekends. We hide them in the back of a van and nip them past security at night.

I'm finding it hard to adjust back to a normal life as I'm still a bit wild and have come off drugs very fast. I can also be paranoid, waiting for something to go wrong, as it normally does when I'm around. Bobby's getting restless as well: he went abroad for the high life and a change of scenery and we're now back working in the UK – and in a place as dreary as Dundee if not worse, only now without his friends.

One night I'm feeling particularly edgy. I'm sitting in a pub in Preston with Sophie and I'm pissed.

'What are you looking at?' I say if anyone even glances at me.

'What's wrong with you?' Sophie asks me.

And before I can stop myself I tell her everything. It all comes flooding out, everything about my childhood, about how my parents split up when I was ten months old and how me and Tommy spent the next three years being snatched by either Mum or Dad in a tug of war. How I told the judge I wanted to be with my dad when I was only four and how for the next twelve years I paid the price for my stupid mistake by being put through daily torture and living hell by my drunken, psychotic father who beat, punched, kicked, bit, strangled, smashed and battered me and then subjected me to hours and hours of mind-bending inquisitions more or less every day of my childhood until the night I paid him back – just ten minutes in return for twelve years of horrific abuse. How I then walked out and went to live with my mum who I'd hardly even seen between the ages of four and ten.

Sophie just sits there saying nothing. She can hardly believe what I'm telling her at first, but she knows how hard it's been for me to open up to her like that and that everything I've just told her is the plain, honest truth.

'I always saw you as this bright, funny guy,' she says.

She is overwhelmed, but at the same time I think she now wants to save me – *you'll do for my summer project*, she must be thinking.

But I know it's more than that. For me to let my guard down and tell her this is huge and I can only do it because I know she's a really genuine, kind and caring person. If you met her you'd know what I mean.

And even now as I'm telling her about what I went through I still can't understand why someone like her, as beautiful as her, would go for someone like me.

The work has finished at the holiday camp and Bobby decides to go back to Scotland, as he's never felt the love he first thought he had for Katie. I'm getting restless as well, because I've moved back to the small room in the halls with no job while Sophie is at university. I have too much time to think again as I'm alone most of the day and I never really wanted to move back to the UK. It was meant to be a holiday but has turned back into a life.

I sit down with Sophie one night and tell her I'm going back abroad for a while, as I can't handle not working and her being at uni all day. I know it's going to break both of our hearts but I can't be alone for more than a couple of hours as I start thinking about my childhood – my demons are never far away.

'I'm coming with you,' she says instantly.

'Don't be crazy, you can't leave university.'

'I don't care about uni, I just want to be with you.'

'It's your life! And I don't want to be responsible for ruining it.'

274

She's crying now. 'It's *my* life, you can't make decisions for me, I'm coming with you.'

I have never had someone love me so much that they would give up everything to be with me. I don't know if it's me being selfish or lonely or even flattered but I eventually agree and promise to look after her.

There's still the issue of telling Sophie's parents and we have to travel back to Cheshire to break the news that I, some nutcase from Scotland, am taking their precious little girl away to a foreign country for the summer.

I have never met two nicer people in my life. Her dad reminds me of Tom Selleck, the one in *Three Men and a Baby* – a proper family man who loves his wife and kids, and even though his daughter is getting involved with someone who he probably thinks is the worst thing to have happened to her, he still supports her in any decision she makes and in my eyes that's true love from a real father. Even though we've never met before and he doesn't know me, he gives me a big hug and says, 'You'll look after my daughter.'

Her mother is an older version of Sophie looks-wise and her parents seem to be equal in every decision in life they make. Sophie's happiness seems to be the main agenda in their life even though I still get a feeling that they personally think I'm not right for their daughter. But whatever makes Sophie happy is good enough for them. I only hope I can live up to their expectations as I still have very mixed feelings about where my life is going.

*   *   *

So off I go again, only this time I have a girlfriend to look after – and I find it hard to look after myself. We move to another part of Spain, but then things go downhill really fast. While I'm out looking for a job I leave Sophie at a hostel for a couple of hours and tell her to keep the door locked as there are always weirdos and thieves living in those kinds of places.

When I get back Sophie is crying.

'I went to the toilet and I was only gone for two minutes.'

'What's happened, what is it?' I'm now really panicking.

'Everything's gone. Travellers' cheques, credit cards,' she sobs. 'Everything's been stolen.'

Luckily I have the passports in my pocket. But yet again my new life seems to have turned to disaster and this time I've dragged Sophie into my constant run of bad luck.

I get a job bringing people into a club and one night I'm offered some ecstasy. I'm soon back into my own selfish ways, forgetting the promise I made Sophie's father. This isn't because of my difficult childhood, this is down to my weak, addictive personality.

I'm out in the clubs all night, hours after she's given up and gone home, back to whatever apartment we're staying in. Sophie's watching me as I literally try to kill myself with drugs and drink, and my raging temper keeps flaring at the slightest provocation. I'm on a self-destruct mission and Sophie hasn't a clue how to deal with it at such a young age. I can't look after myself and will never let anyone get too close, so what chance does an eighteen year old have of changing me, even with the love she seems to feel for me?

I'm still too young to be in a relationship, or at least I think I must be. I still don't trust anybody and find it very hard to believe that somebody that age loves me. I don't want somebody tagging along when I've got all this baggage and I don't want to hurt her. And finally, to be really honest, I think so little of myself I don't think she can be worth much if she cares about someone like me. I can't trust myself so why should she trust me? It's like that old Groucho Marx joke, 'I wouldn't want to join any club that would have me as a member.'

We break up even though it feels as though our relationship has hardly even begun. After just one month of living together she's moved out. I don't even know who finally ends it, me or her. All I know is that I'm a disaster zone and if she'd stayed with me any longer I would have dragged her down with me.

Why am I doing this? Why can't I accept love from someone who I know is the best thing in my life? These are questions I ask myself again and again in the following days and weeks, while I have another drink in another bar and snort another line of coke.

After eight months of this mayhem and misery Sophie goes back home to England. She's out of my life for good.

I can hardly believe it. I've thrown away my one chance of happiness. I don't even want to think about it and I try to tell myself I'm better off on my own. I've always been a loner at heart, I say to myself, and I don't need anyone else.

I'm like the Littlest Hobo, the lone wolf. I'm like my dog Bonnie, except that she was trusting and loyal. I'm like Dad in a way that I hate – I'll turn on anyone who shows me love and destroy everything in my path.

A few weeks later I leave Spain and go to see some lads from Tyrone in Ireland that I have met up with during this period.

I just can't settle anywhere or with anyone. I'm destined to be a loner, pushing my body to the limit and leaving a trail of destruction behind me.

When I arrive in Ireland in 2000 at the age of 24 I make a promise to myself never to take drugs again or drink alcohol to the extent I have been for the past few years. And this time I mean it.

If my time with Sophie has taught me anything, it's that I don't want to be that guy who doesn't trust anyone or let anyone get close to him. Sophie made me want to change: if I can't live with myself how would I ever be able to live with anyone else?

Over the next three years in Ireland my life is turned around. I'm back playing football, going to the gym, and I make a lot of good friends. I have the odd hiccup – I'm completely drug-free but there's still the very occasional night out in town when I get drunk – but nothing major, as I have truly started learning to control my fists and my anger.

A Voice in the Wilderness, a Face in the Crowd

I'm now working as a barman in a seriously posh hotel in Balls Bridge in Dublin, the Herbert Park. I'm enjoying life again, like the times when I was younger with Tommy and Bobby.

I hardly ever have any arguments with anyone – except on a football pitch. Referees are the new enemy, but you can always shake hands at the end as it's now about passion and not violence.

The only problem at this time is something that has been eating me up inside for the past three years. It's the guilt and remorse I still feel – guilt over what I have done to Sophie and remorse that I have thrown it all away.

My guilt keeps nagging away at me – for taking Sophie out of her university course, for promising her a life I would never be able to give her and for being so selfish. I should have stopped her coming with me back to Spain as I was in no fit frame of mind to have someone to look after when I couldn't even take care of myself.

After all this time, I still miss her. I can't seem to get her out of my head, and the memory of her seems to follow me around; every day. I look around and there's a heartache following me.

She's been the only good thing I can remember from this hazy part of my life. I still love her and every woman that I am with knows it as well. If I have arguments with any woman I'm seeing, I'll compare them to Sophie.

'Sophie wouldn't do that, Sophie would never have said that.'

It's driving me crazy as I have done something worse than Dad ever did to me. I have broken a young girl's heart.

I never have a number, any address or any idea of where Sophie might be living, and I have no idea whether she would talk to me again even if I did find her. I just want to talk to her to apologise for the pain I have caused her. I also pray every week that she is happy and that she's found someone to take care of her.

And I'm always thinking, maybe I'll meet someone like Sophie again. And if I can get myself back to normal and if it happens again, I won't blow it this time.

I'm older and wiser – though not that much older or wiser – but maybe because of what I've been through, when people look at me they seem to know that I've had a hard life just by talking to me. I seem a lot older than my 27 years. It's obviously to do with my upbringing: even at 21 when I moved abroad people always thought of me as older. But now, if there's any kind of violence around me, I walk away. I want to be a different person. I'm doing it for myself. And for someone like Sophie who might come into my life. I'm doing it for her, that person.

I'm out in town in Dublin. It's around two o'clock in the afternoon, and me and Bjorn, a friend from Sweden, are shopping for clothes. We've given up hope of finding anything as the shops are beginning to close up for the day. I look at my watch and then have to step to the side so as not to bump into people coming in the opposite direction.

As I look up to apologise, I see her standing there in front of me, about six inches away – and my heart explodes.

She is holding hands with a guy but we are now staring at each other in shock.

I can't believe it – her beautiful face only inches from me. Then she lets go his hand as we lunge at each other. I'm squeezing her harder than I have ever held anyone in my life.

'Sophie!'

'Charlie!'

Everything around me has disappeared. I stand back to have another look at her, still holding her hands.

'How are you, what are you doing here?'

By this time her boyfriend must be thinking, *Who the hell is this?*

'I'm on a weekend break! Oh! This is Steve.'

I shake his hand – well, squeeze as he's standing with my Sophie. We talk very briefly then say our goodbyes. I walk in one direction, she goes the other.

I can't think. I can't see straight. And my heart is still pounding out of my shirt.

'Who was that, Charlie?' asks Bjorn.

'The woman I should be married to.'

'Oh! Was that *the* Sophie?'

'Yeah that was her!'

'I didn't know before what you meant when you said you were stupid, but stupid is the wrong word – I would say insane!'

'Thanks for that, mate.'

I still can't believe I've seen her and let her go without telling her I'm sorry, but I'm glad she's OK and looking fantastic.

Actually, she's looking incredible. I just can't believe how incredible she looks.

As I walk along the road my head is all over the place.

'Why don't you go and find her,' Bjorn says. 'Tell her how you feel.'

'No, she's with someone. Just leave it, mate—'

'*Charlie!*'

I feel someone jump on my back and wrap their arms around me.

It's Sophie – she has come back to find me.

I can't help it. I start to cry.

'Sophie, I still love you, I'm sorry. I was an idiot. I'm really, really sorry.'

'I still love you as well,' she says.

I'm sobbing now and so is she, and we're kissing and hugging and wild horses couldn't tear us apart.

I feel at this moment that my life has turned full circle and my heart wants to burst with happiness. I do have some unanswered questions about my time on this planet still, like: Who is the guardian angel that keeps saving me? Who keeps answering my prayers? Who controls my fate? Is it my angel from above and why in this year, on this month, on this day, at this time, in this place do we end up six inches from each other?

I will probably never know but for me I don't care. My Sophie is here.

And to be honest with you, the only time in my life I've felt as good as this was when Dundee United beat Barcelona at Tannadice.

Epilogue

We walked over to a hotel and chatted about how much we had missed each other, and how sorry I was for what I had done, still holding on to each other's jackets, in case someone stole the other one away. She had told Steve that she had to be alone for a minute and came and found me.

We exchanged numbers, said our goodbyes and kept in touch for the next six months. I was over the moon. Sophie finished with Steve when she got home, and started visiting me in Ireland as she had now become an air hostess, and had free flights to everywhere. She could see that I'd stopped taking drugs and stopped drinking so we decided to start afresh, all over again. A clean slate, as if we had just met.

The first time Sophie visited me in Dublin, we went out for a meal, then a drink, catching up on lost time. I told her how sorry I was for what I had done to her; how things had changed in my head. I wasn't that aggressive thug I used to be.

We had a good night, talking about what we had been up to for the past few years. She kept commenting on how different I looked and how calm I had become, as she knew me as hyperactive, someone who would be running around a dance floor, who never sat and had a serious conversation for two minutes. And I wasn't looking around the room any more, waiting for trouble. When we had a dance now, my eyes were fixed only on her.

I made another life-changing choice after that. I was going to move back with Sophie, as she had been the one making all the sacrifices up until then. I wanted to prove to her that I was as much in love with her as she was with me.

But before we could move on with our lives there was one thing I needed to do. I had decided to go back to Scotland to see Dad, and to let Sophie meet him too. I flew into Liverpool airport and arranged to meet Sophie at Preston Station. We couldn't risk meeting in Chester in case I was spotted by one of her family as our being back together was still top secret. Her parents only knew me as the guy that broke their little girl's heart.

Then I took her to see the man who had made my childhood a misery and who turned me into the monster I used to be. She was curious what he was like as I had told her everything that he had done to me. I think she was a bit scared too, but that was outweighed by anger.

He's still living in that semi-detached in St Fillans Road, the one I walked out of after I beat him up for the first and last time.

But he isn't the big strong man I remember – he's now a frail old man with grey hair, a bit wobbly on his legs, with an old-looking face. He's changed his bottle of vodka for cider now, and the house smells of old people, a musty kind of smell. My reaction is different to what I thought it would be. I kind of feel sorry for him, as he has clearly tried to drink himself to death, probably because of all those years of guilt. I'm glad I never killed him back then, as he has done a better job of it to himself than I could ever have done.

He isn't as threatening as I remember him either. After chatting, mainly small talk, we decide to watch a video on the VCR and choose *Braveheart*, one of his favourites – and still one of mine, to be honest.

As he sits on the floor watching the movie, he's crying, 'Look what they English bastards did to oor women and kids. Bastards, fuckin' bastards!'

'Watch yir mooth, Dad. Sophie's English.'

'Sorry son. She's aright.'

I think he has run out of anger and is now depressed beyond belief. Drink does that to you. Drugs are illegal but alcohol has probably ruined more lives than anything else on the planet and it's still available over the counter. I spent my childhood witnessing first hand the effects of what alcohol did to my dad and what he then did to me in turn.

But I think Sophie is quite shocked at the fact that he is so small and weak, as she is expecting some huge evil man. She has seen me take on three or four lads at a time, and this grey-haired old man is nothing compared to them. Sophie's anger has turned to pity too, and she's gazing at me with a sad look on her face.

'Is he OK?'

Dad is now swaying from side to side and shaking.

'Don't you worry aboot me pal, just dinna use all mi toilet roll,' he chuckles away to himself. At least his hearing is still OK.

I don't know what I'm expecting from him. Maybe I think he's going to apologise for what he did to me all those years ago. But he can hardly remember yesterday, never mind my childhood.

Or maybe I think that seeing him again will help me come to terms with all that rage in me, even if I have calmed down over the last two or three years. But seeing him now only leaves me with a sense of pity. Not for him – he's way beyond feeling sorry for. And not for myself – I've exhausted all my self-pity in too many late nights in Spanish bars.

But pity for the waste of it all – all those years when he and I could have been happy together, when he could have been a real dad to me like Sophie's dad, caring for his children, cherishing their lives, and happy for their existence, instead of what he's turned into – a shrunken shell of a man, consumed by his own anger, and demented and destroyed by years of addiction to alcohol. And when he couldn't vent all his rage on Mum, me, Bonnie and all his girlfriends, he's probably turned it all in on himself.

He just sits there drunk, trying to make a joke of everything on his own, in his three-bedroom house. Tommy has gone up to see him, to try and get him to stop drinking. But Dad doesn't care any more; he just wants to die.

It's sad really; he chose the wrong road and I nearly did too. I guess he wasn't as strong as I was after all. Maybe he couldn't handle the things his father did to him. Or maybe he just didn't care. And I'm not hanging around to find out. It's all far too late to make any difference anyway.

I don't feel guilty for saying what I said the night I walked out of his house when I was sixteen, when I told him I didn't care less if he lived or died. When I was less than four years old I was in a tug of war between my mum and my dad. I told the judge I wanted to be with my dad. It was a bad choice, but then again, four-year-old kids aren't very good at multiple-choice tests. And besides, I paid the price for my bad choice for years and years to come. But hey, that's life.

But that's all in the past. I've got my life back and if there is such a thing as karma – and I believe there is – all debts have been paid.

The Nipper

All the king's horses and all the king's men
Couldn't put Charlie together again.
But Sophie did.

Afterword

So what has happened to everyone?

Sophie and I left Scotland and headed for England. We met up again in Preston to make sure things were going to be OK between us. She went to tell her parents the news that she was getting back with the boy who had promised to look after her and let her down. I felt so sorry for her. But whatever they may have said to her, they must have eventually given her their blessings to carry on seeing me.

The other reason for going back there with her was to erase all the memories since the last time we left Preston – the years we spent apart and the eight months of hell I put her through. I started a double-glazing job in Lancashire; I was a conservatory fabricator – well, that's what I told the person who hired me. I could pick things up very quickly, as I would watch other people and copy what they did.

Preston was good for me, as I was getting prepared for life in Cheshire. And it would give Sophie's parents time to get used to the idea of us being back together. After six months of living in Preston, we moved to Cheshire so Sophie could be close to her family, and I could spend the rest of my life making it up to her and to them, which I'm still doing.

As for me, my anger seems to have disappeared and, after all those false starts and broken promises to myself and Sophie, I have finally, truly turned my life around. I will never even look at a drug again.

I still have problems. I'm more settled in myself, but I don't even know now whether my head is straight down the middle. I still have split feelings about everything. Every decision I make, even now, I still question the things that I do, from everyday decisions to small moral choices. I hate letting people down and I'll take it out on myself. But when it gets too much for me, Sophie will just tell me to stop being daft, and I calm down.

To be honest I often feel the fact that my life has been turned around is down to pure luck in meeting Sophie – though I still believe that she was sent to me from heaven. In the last five years Sophie and I have bought a house together, got married and gone to the Maldives on our honeymoon. A lot of people from my past came to my wedding, like Blake, Mum's second husband, and Calum, my old nutcase school friend and partner in crime.

Garry, the older brother of my late cousin Shane was my best man. Shane was a true friend and an exceptional person who inspired me to keep going. He died recently of cancer of the oesophagus, aged thirty. Not a day goes by that I don't think about him. Shane is the reason I believe there is life after death. If God, or whoever is upstairs, can take someone like him off the earth then I know for a fact that it doesn't end here. If I can be half the man in my later years that he was in his life, I'll never be stuck for friends.

Paul, Mandy's son and still my closest friend, was my other best man. I couldn't believe how nice Paul and his brother Peter were to my dad while I was away from Dundee and out of the country, going up to his house every now and again to keep an eye on him. Dad was such a nice guy when he was sober, and he was also able to manipulate people in a way that I will never be able to explain – I've tried throughout this book, but it's still a mystery to me. If you can tell me why the whole German nation followed Adolf Hitler, I'll tell you why Paul cared for the well-being of my dad. And as I said earlier, Paul had mainly blanked out the rest of what went on.

The first time Sophie and I went away again, which was on our honeymoon, I was anxious and apprehensive that I would repeat the disastrous fiasco of our eight months in Spain. But the honeymoon turned out to be perfect, and after the Maldives we've had other holidays together, with no problems.

I have passed my driving test at the fifth attempt; though I failed four times in England, I went back to Dundee to see if I knew the roads any better and it worked! I now own my own business, and Sophie and I are expecting our first child. I can't wait to see his or her little face when he or she comes into the world. One thing I know for certain: I will never treat my children the way Dad treated me.

Now that we're going to have a kid and I've felt the baby kicking through Sophie's belly and can feel its hand running across my hand through her stomach, I just do not, and never will in a million years, understand how Dad could have done what he did to me and a four-foot-tall woman and my dog Bonnie.

You'd have to be pretty sick in the head to think that I deserved all the punishment he gave me because I was a naughty boy. If I heard a little kid saying *please please please* for hours I would smash the door down, phone the police, do anything in my power to stop it, but people back then just seemed to accept it.

Somebody said to me once, he must have had a hard time on his own bringing me up. Bringing me up? He didn't bring me up. He dragged me up. He beat me up, he smashed me up. I do not get it and I never will. All I can say is that I think there must be a bad gene, a cut-off switch that's gone, a chemical imbalance. Maybe it's the mixture of Scottish and Irish: *that*, as a good friend of mine once said, *will do it!*

My granddad had it and my dad had it. But thank God I don't have it. If I ever lifted my hand to a woman or child – which I've never done – I'd wake up the next day and I'd leave.

While Sophie and I were on our honeymoon, I received a phone call from my cousin, telling me that Dad had died. I didn't know what to feel. I felt numb. Maybe I felt nothing, or maybe I felt everything, I just don't know. Sophie suggested going home, but left it for me to decide. I felt that we both needed the break and should try to enjoy the rest of our honeymoon after everything we had been through.

On returning from the Maldives I received a telephone call from Tommy who was in prison at the time. After Dad's death his house was about to be repossessed by the council. As Tommy had some belongings in there he asked if I could go to Dundee and collect them and take them over to a friend's house. While I was there, collecting Tommy's things, I found a single sheet of paper, face down on a hi-fi speaker. I don't know why but I turned it over to read it. In what seemed to be drunken, squiggly handwriting it simply said:

I love you, Tommy and Charlie.
Dad

All I can say at this point is: what a waste of a life. When he was sober he couldn't face the person he was and the things he had done so he, literally, bottled out.

I miss the good times with him, when we went camping, and went to see Dundee United and when he told jokes, because sober he was hilarious. I miss the person he was when other people were around or when he wasn't drinking or hitting me. I miss the Good Jock who died many years ago – years before the shell of a man that remained of my father drank himself to death. When I think about him now I think he did love me, but that he was twisted, so any love he showed me quickly turned to hate, probably because he hated himself.

The common attitude of those who knew Dad casually – or thought they knew him well – like the men who came into contact with him in the pubs of Dundee, was 'Good old Jock, he's got a bit of a drink problem, but he's alright.' And they loved him because he could be one of the funniest guys in the world. But he couldn't talk to anyone without turning it into a joke. I was like that too. I couldn't hold a conversation with anyone without taking the mick. Lots of people used to say it to me. I think Sophie has helped me to listen more.

Uncle Danny died the year before, also with liver failure from drinking, aged fifty. Danny had a kid by this woman in a place outside Dundee who eventually went off with the kid. She hadn't seen any of the family for twenty-five years and I went four or five years ago up to this place in the hills of Scotland and knocked on her door and found her and introduced her back into the family.

I discovered later that when Dad used to say I wasn't his son, but Danny's, he was just saying it to be malicious. He said it to get in my head and when I told Mum about it she laughed, and said, 'Jesus Christ, I must have slept with Danny twice because you and Tommy are identical!' And she's right of course. Physically Tommy and I could be twins!

Mum and I are like best friends now, catching up on all the years we missed out on together. We're very close and more alike than anyone in the family. She still looks the same, a little more tanned nowadays, but young at heart and she still goes out to clubs. She's still energetic: she's always worked and continues to this day. Physically I take after her and everyone says they can see me in my mum and vice versa – personality and looks.

Tommy went back to Dundee to live, and ended up spending more time in prison than he was out. He's living in another country now – Barbados or Brazil, he moves around a lot – but he's chilled out for the first time in his life.

Bobby is married and has a little boy with a lovely wife, but is serving a prison sentence at the moment for police assault; you may not think it but he has calmed down a lot, apart from this one hiccup in the past five years.

Calum Patterson is a drummer in a band at weekends and has a window-cleaning business. Both Dad's long-term girlfriends have now married good men and their kids now have kids of their own.

Life is too short to be holding grudges or thinking about the past, and anyone from any walk of life can turn things around if they want it badly enough. Or meet the right woman.

This book is not a plea for sympathy; it's an apology to everyone who had the misfortune to meet me at that time of my life, and to ask that you think before you choose your life path. Don't make your upbringing an excuse to ruin other people's lives. Don't abuse women and children, don't take drugs, don't get that drunk that you don't know what you're doing, don't let things fester inside you.

Never give up. Always remember who your friends are, and family. Wear your heart on your sleeve. Choose football, choose shopping, choose a house in the quiet countryside, choose lying on the beach drinking cocktails in the sun, choose love. Because whatever you choose in life, the choices will affect the next generation of little people we bring into the world, and your future.

Luckily for me Sophie chose her heart instead of her head. I think fate chose me.

Acknowledgement

I would like to thank Sir Alex Ferguson, Manager of Manchester United. If it wasn't for him I probably would never have written this book.

I was flying back from the Scotland versus Ukraine match recently (when Scotland whipped them, may I add). I was still feeling a bit rough on the flight from the night before, sitting against the window in one of two seats, the other one being empty. I was leaning with my head on my hand waiting for take-off when someone sat down beside me, and nudged my arm off the arm rest.

When I turned my head, to my amazement, Sir Alex Ferguson was sitting there right next to me. I didn't speak to him straightaway as I didn't want to pester him, as most people probably do. So I put my head back against the window and tried to get some sleep. It just wasn't happening, as my head was banging from the party the night before.

It was about ten minutes into the flight when I looked down and saw that Alex was reading a book, I think it was called *Stalingrad*, or something like that. He was nodding off and I thought to myself, let me borrow it as it's obviously helping you get to sleep. The trolley dolly was on her rounds and approaching us fast.

'Tea, coffee anyone?'

'Yea love,' I said, as she got to our row, 'can I have a chicken and stuffing sandwich and a coffee please?' Then I nudged Alex in the arm. 'Do ya want a brew, Alex?'

'No I'm alright son,' he said opening his eyes, probably thinking I was some kind of nut.

We got chatting after that about the game and horses and stuff. He was an absolute gentleman, really down to earth and normal. I still threw in a few of my comical comments like 'if Tevez or Rooney get injured he should give me a call', as I was top scorer in most of the crap amateur teams that I had played for. I think that probably confirmed what he was thinking.

We had now got on to the subject of books. He had asked me if I read them and explained a little bit about the one he was reading. I wanted to say yes, as I didn't want him to think I was an idiot, but I couldn't lie to him, as he might have asked me which ones I'd read, then I would have to lock myself in the toilet with embarrassment for the rest of the flight. He advised me to try and read books on something I was interested in, as I have suffered from insomnia for many years now, and find it impossible to sleep at night.

That night when I arrived home I told Sophie about meeting him and what he had said about reading books.

'I've been telling you that for years, but you never listened to me.'

She had, but I have never really had the patience to read. The only book I had ever even attempted to read was Billy Connolly's life story, and I only managed to get half way through that.

I have always been interested in real life, hearing about actual things that have happened, so I read a book that my wife was reading called *The Kid*.

When I had finished it, it took me back to my childhood and how intense and horrifying compared to most people's it was. And how eventful it was for a thirty-two-year-old man.

So I would like to say thank you to you, Alex, for inspiring me to read, as I would never have written this book if we had never met.